Oh Scandal! Oh Ruin!

"Oh, my lord," she cried. "You are ill!" She fished in her reticule, took out a bottle of cologne and a clean handkerchief, and proceeded to bathe his temples. Esther had a very strong maternal instinct. When he shuddered and murmured, "Oh, such death, such suffering. Will it never end?" she knew immediately he was in the grip of a nightmare. Forgetting about the staring, curious crowd, forgetting Lord Guy was a rake and a libertine, she put her arms round him and hugged him as she hugged the children when they had bad dreams and said softly, "Shhh! You are not at war. You are here with Esther. Everything is all right."

Gradually his eyes focussed on the beautiful face so close to his own. He did not know where he was and he did not care. He wrapped his arms around her and kissed her passionately on the mouth, more passionately than he had ever kissed a woman in the whole of his life.

"WHAT MAKES THIS REGENCY NOVEL UNUSUAL IS THE PART THE STAFF PLAYS IN THE EVENTS... WARMHEARTED...READING."
—*The Baton Rouge Sunday Magazine*

Also by Marion Chesney

RAKE'S PROGRESS

Book 4 of
A House for the Season

MARION CHESNEY

ST. MARTIN'S PRESS/NEW YORK

RAKE'S PROGRESS

Copyright © 1987 by Marion Chesney

Library of Congress Catalog Card Number: 87-4407

ISBN: 0-312-91036-3

Printed in the United States of America

First St. Martin's Press mass market edition/April 1988

10 9 8 7 6 5 4 3 2 1

For Ita Ali,
Maria Browne, and
Jane Wibberley

Chapter One

When late I attempted your pity to move,
What made you so deaf to my prayers?
Perhaps it was right to dissemble your love,
But—why did you kick me downstairs?

—ISAAC BICKERSTAFFE

Reputed to be haunted, damned as unlucky, a tall thin town house at Number 67 Clarges Street in London's Mayfair, nonetheless, on that spring day of 1810, looked as if the curse had been lifted and the tide of ill fortune had turned.

It belonged to the Duke of Pelham, who was only dimly aware of its existence. He owned a great deal of other property. The letting of it, and the employing of the staff, was the job of Jonas Palmer, the duke's agent, cheat, bully, and liar. He paid the servants low wages, charged his master higher wages, and slipped the difference into his coat pocket.

The servants, either because they had gained bad reputations—unjustly—or because they stayed at Number 67 out of loyalty to the other members of the staff, continued to pray for a new tenant every Season. A tenant meant parties, routs, and suppers, and all those festivities meant lashings of good food and tips. They all put their tips in the Vail Box so that, when they had sufficient, they would buy a pub and become independent of the frightful Palmer.

Hard times and resentment of Palmer had welded them together into an odd sort of family. Head of the family was the butler, Rainbird. After him came housekeeper, Mrs. Middleton; cook, Angus MacGregor; and, next down the line, the effeminate footman, Joseph. There were a chambermaid, Jenny; a housemaid, Alice; and little Lizzie, the scullery maid. Dave, who had been rescued from his miserable life as a climbing boy by Rainbird, was the pot boy.

On that fine sunny spring day, they were all assembled in the hall, the women crackling with starch and the men in their best liveries. They were awaiting the arrival of a new tenant, and a tenant who showed all the signs of being open-handed.

He was Lord Guy Carlton, younger son of the Earl of Cramworth. He had been fighting in the wars against Napoleon for some time and was being invalided home. Palmer had said sourly that from his letters it appeared my lord had every intention of kicking up his heels and had said he meant to hold many parties.

The optimism of the servants seemed to have communicated itself to the house and banished the ghosts. The ninth Duke of Pelham had hanged himself there; a murderer had fallen to his death there sometime after killing one of the tenants' daughters. But now the narrow black town house looked fresh and new. Even the two iron dogs chained on the step outside had been polished so hard by Dave that sunlight sparkled on their metal flanks.

Spring flowers decorated the rooms, which smelled pleasantly of beeswax and lavender.

As they gathered in the hall to greet their new, if temporary, master, the servants talked amiably to each other, not observing that rigid caste system of the servants' hall —much more strict than any of the social divisions abovestairs. As soon as Lord Guy arrived, they would remember their places in the pecking order.

Mrs. Middleton, spinster daughter of a curate and fallen on hard times—the "Mrs." was a courtesy title— smoothed down her best black silk gown with nervous fingers.

"I do wonder what Lord Guy will be like," she said for what seemed like the hundredth time.

"He must have settled in his ways, although he is not married," said Rainbird, the butler, his sparkling grey eyes set in his comedian's face darting here and there to make sure everything was in order. "I looked up the peerage. He is thirty-five, long past sowing his wild oats."

"I wonder if he is handsome," said Alice dreamily. Alice, the housemaid, was a beautiful blonde, slow-moving and languorous.

"Eh wish he wasn't bringing his own sarvant," said Joseph, the footman, in his mincing, affected tones. "Strange sarvants cause trouble, if you esk me."

"Nobody asked you, you clown," snapped Rainbird, who had contracted a hopeless passion two years before for a visiting lady's maid and had not yet got over it.

Unabashed, Joseph picked a piece of lint from his velvet sleeve and went on, "Besides, I think it is not quait the *thing* to have all of us to greet him." He looked contemptuously at Lizzie and Dave, who were waiting to take their places at the bottom of the reception line.

"You disgust me, you jessamy," growled Angus MacGregor, the fiery-tempered Highland cook. "Lizzie is more of a lady than you'll ever be a gentleman."

Lizzie, the scullery maid, looked distressed. She had fallen in love with the footman when she had first arrived, and loved him still, although she was not blind to his faults.

"Mayhap his servant will be a great soldier brute," said Dave cheerfully, "who likes picking fights with footmen."

"Don't," said Lizzie, distressed. "We've hardly quarreled all winter. Don't let's start now."

"Silly Lizzie," said quick and dark Jenny, the chambermaid. "We're all that excited. And this is the first winter we've passed where we've all had enough to eat and enough coals to warm us. I know we're going to have a wonderful Season. What's the matter now, Liz?" she demanded crossly, seeing a shadow lurking in the little scullery maid's eyes. "You ain't gone and had one of your presmonishuns."

"I only feel," said Lizzie cautiously, "that a gentleman who has spent all of his youth in battle won't want a quiet life."

"Shouldn't ha' taught her to read and write," jeered Joseph. "Education addles the brain." He had taken to picking on Lizzie of late, a nasty habit everyone thought he had given up.

"Aye, weel," said Angus MacGregor, "you're the most addled brain here and you can barely read a book."

"Shhh!" said Rainbird. "I hear a carriage approaching!"

They all fell into line.

Rainbird threw open the door. But the carriage went on past.

"Not yet," he said, disappointed. "I wonder what's keeping his lordship!"

"I suppose we had best be on our way," said Lord Guy Carlton regretfully, putting down his empty glass. He and

his friend, Mr. Tommy Roger—nicknamed the Jolly Roger
—had stopped to take some refreshment.

"No hurry," said Mr. Roger. "Let's have another bottle. You look as fit as a flea, Guy. If the colonel could see
you now, he'd have you posted back on the next ship."

"Go back when I'm ready," said Lord Guy lazily. "Another bottle it is. That fever was the best thing that happened to us for ages. I don't know about you, but it made
up my mind for me."

"Thought you'd never leave the battlefield, you old
war horse," said Mr. Roger affectionately. "You swore
you'd fight on until you saw the last of Boney. Don't know
how you stood it all these years."

"Don't know either," agreed Lord Guy amiably. He
pulled a pretty serving maid onto his lap, kissed her on the
lips, and told her to bring another bottle of the best. The
girl went off, giggling.

"Don't waste your energies on serving maids," said
Mr. Roger. "I plan to treat myself to the best high-flier in
London."

"Only one?" mocked Lord Guy. "I plan to have 'em by
the dozen."

The two men, who were roughly the same age, made
an odd contrast. Mr. Roger was squat and dark, with a head
of tough wiry black hair. He was still in his scarlet regimen-
tals, looking as odd without his horse as a reeling sailor on
dry land without his ship, for his legs were pronouncedly
bandy.

Lord Guy was tall, slim, and fair. His high-nosed, rakish face was lightly tanned, and his merry blue eyes under
their drooping lids had a habitual devil-may-care look.

He was dressed in civilian clothes, blue morning coat
with plaited buttons, leather breeches, and top-boots. His
cravat was intricately tied and starched. In contrast to all

this understudied elegance, his waistcoat was an embroidered riot of gold and scarlet birds of paradise.

As they broached the new bottle, an amiable silence fell between the two friends.

They were sitting in the garden of an inn at Croydon. Crocuses were peeping up through the grass, and the branches of the trees, still bare of leaves, stretched up to the pale blue sky.

A huge puffy cloud passed overhead, reminding Lord Guy of the ship that had borne him home. Home! How odd that sounded. Home would be a rented house in Town for a few months. His conscience told him he would be back at the battlefront as soon as the Season had ended.

He could have stayed. His fever, though violent, had soon abated, leaving him weak and listless. The voyage home had been calm and restful. His health was almost immediately restored.

But for the moment, he was sick of war and bloodshed. He wanted to surround himself with the prettiest women in Town and kick up all those silly pranks that single gentlemen indulged in. He planned not to let one serious thought enter his head until it was time to go back.

He did not plan to marry. Women, like fine wine, were to be savoured and treated with respect, and, like wine, there was a tempting variety to look forward to.

An hour and another bottle later, Mr. Roger idly remarked that the sun was setting and the day had lost its warmth.

"This house I've taken for us," remarked Lord Guy, rising to his feet, "some fellow told me it was unlucky."

"Must have been a gambler," said Mr. Roger, nodding wisely and then finding to his surprise that he could not stop nodding. "They're a supperstish . . . sushersh . . ."

"Superstitious," said Lord Guy with a smile. "You're foxed, Tommy."

"Am I, b'Gad! Lovely."

"Where's that man of mine, Manuel?"

"Try raising an eyebrow. He's always lurking about. Makes my flesh creep."

Darkness had fallen on Number 67 Clarges Street. The oil lamps and candles had been lit. Mrs. Middleton, weary with the long wait, was asleep in a chair in the hall, her large starched and frilled cap casting a shadow over her face, which wore its habitually frightened, anxious look even in repose. Joseph was cleaning his nails. The Moocher, the kitchen cat, was the only thing in the household that looked alert as it sat facing the door with a comic air of expectancy.

"Ah'm off down the stairs," grumbled Angus MacGregor wearily. "I dinnae think he's going tae come now." He took off his white skull-cap, exposing a head of flaming red hair, fished inside the cap, produced the end of a cheroot, and lit it with a candle.

"Then take that nasty-smelling thing with you, Angus," said Rainbird crossly. "Jenny's been sprinkling rose water in all the rooms, and what's the point of it if you're going to stink the place up?"

"Someone's coming," said Lizzie.

"I've opened that door about a hundred times today," said Rainbird. "It's just a carriage going back from a rout."

Angus was just making for the backstairs when there came a brisk tattoo at the door. Knocking at a door in London was an art, like drumming. The number of knocks and the violence and rhythm with which they were performed denoted the importance of the visitor. This tattoo was sounded with all the vigour and verve of a Royal footman.

7

Angus threw his cheroot into his cap and crammed it on his head. Mrs. Middleton awoke with a start. Rainbird pulled down his waistcoat and made for the door while all the servants formed a line in the hall behind him.

He swung open the door. A slim, supercilious manservant looked at him contemptuously. "You take the time, fellow, do you not?" he remarked with exquisite insolence. He stood aside as two gentlemen mounted the steps.

"Well, this isn't too bad," said Lord Guy, strolling into the hall with Mr. Tommy Roger. "Not bad at all," he said, one wicked blue eye rolling in Alice's direction.

Rainbird began introducing the servants. Smoke from the burning cheroot was beginning to send curls of smoke out from under the cook's cap. Rainbird banged MacGregor on the head when he felt he was unobserved in the hope of extinguishing it. When he came to the women, Lord Guy smiled charmingly on Mrs. Middleton, grinned at Jenny, winked at Lizzie, caught Alice around the waist, drew her to him, and planted a lazy, caressing kiss full on her mouth.

Alice looked up at him in a dazed way.

"My lord," said Rainbird repressively, "you will wish to see your rooms."

Mrs. Middleton took Alice, who was standing with her mouth open, firmly by the hand and led her downstairs, signalling to the other women to follow.

"Draw me a bath, will you?" said Lord Guy. "Rainbird, I think you said your name was. This is my servant, Manuel. Look after him. He's a capital chap."

There was a loud crash as Mr. Tommy Roger fell over on the tiled floor and began to snore.

"And black coffee," said Lord Guy. "I do not plan to celebrate my first night in Town alone. Sober Mr. Roger, please, after you have drawn my bath."

"Yes, my lord," said Rainbird woodenly.

"And send that fair-haired beauty up to scrub my back."

"Of course, my lord," said Rainbird, determined to humour him. He was sure Lord Guy was as drunk as his friend and would probably fall asleep in his bath. He led the way upstairs.

The ground floor of the house consisted of front and back parlours, the first floor of a dining room and bedroom. There were two bedrooms above that, and above that, the attics.

With the exception of little Lizzie, who washed herself regularly under the pump, the servants frowned on bathing, thinking it a pernicious practice. It endangered the health, everyone knew that.

So it took some time to prepare my lord's bath, since said bath was in the cellar and full of firewood.

At last Joseph and Rainbird carried its coffin-like shape upstairs. Rainbird told Angus and Dave to help carry the cans of hot water, for he did not want any of the maids to be left alone with Lord Guy who, Rainbird was fast deciding, showed all the signs of being a rake.

In the meantime, Lord Guy had demolished a bottle of champagne. It had served only to deepen the wicked look in his blue eyes and to make him look livelier than ever.

With the help of Manuel, his Spanish servant, he stripped off and sank down into the bath. "Hey, Manuel," he said, "go find me that gorgeous creature."

Manuel bowed, immediately identifying the "gorgeous creature" as Alice.

He walked downstairs and into the servants' hall, where they were all busily discussing the new tenant. Their voices died and they surveyed him in silence. Manuel was small in stature and dressed in black-velvet livery ornamented with pink silk braid. His hair was smooth and black like shiny leather and his skin was olive. His liquid dark eyes were expressionless, his nose was small and thin, and his slightly protruding teeth gave his small mouth a rabbity look.

He beckoned Alice. "My lord wishes you," he said.

Alice blushed and made to step forward.

"No," said Rainbird. "If my lord wishes anything, I shall fetch it, or Joseph here."

The Spanish manservant shrugged. Then he walked towards Alice and seized the maid's hand and started to drag her out. Rainbird leapt forward, wrenched Alice away and gave Manuel a push that sent him flying.

Manuel fished in his pocket and produced a long stiletto knife, which he held to Rainbird's throat. "You," he said to Alice over the butler's shoulder, "go upstairs or I will slit his throat."

A tense silence fell on the servants.

Then Angus MacGregor rolled up his sleeve, stretched one hairy arm around Rainbird, and seized the Spanish manservant by the cravat. Manuel made to stab Rainbird with his knife, but Jenny the chambermaid sank her excellent teeth into his wrist and he let the knife fall with a clatter. MacGregor picked him up and began to shake him to and fro while the Spaniard screamed in terror like a wounded animal.

"What the deuce is going on?" demanded a cold voice from the doorway.

The women began to scream as loudly as Manuel and covered their eyes with their hands, although Mrs. Middleton peeped through her fingers. It was a sight she had not seen before and was not likely to see again.

Lord Guy stood there, dripping water, stark naked.

"Well," he demanded, "what are you doing with my servant?"

"He tried to drag Alice upstairs," said Rainbird. "Then he drew a knife."

"Oh," said Lord Guy blankly. "Don't you want to scrub my back, Alice?"

"No," mumbled Alice.

He shrugged his naked shoulders. "Well, that's that," he said cheerfully. "Manuel, come with me. That knife of yours must never be used again. Oh, Rainbird, get that coffee down Mr. Roger's throat. The night is young, and I am of a mind to enjoy myself."

He strolled out, presenting a view of impertinent, muscled buttocks to the embarrassed servants, with his Spanish shadow at his heels.

"Oh, dear, dear, dear," mourned Rainbird. "What a Season this is going to be. Joseph, you'd best come and help me with Mr. Roger. Angus, bring lots of coffee."

By dint of walking Mr. Roger up and down for about an hour and pouring scalding black coffee down his throat from time to time, they managed to get him upstairs to his bedroom. Lord Guy had taken the large bedroom behind the dining room, so they propelled him into the front bedroom on the floor above.

Rainbird signalled to Joseph to remove Mr. Roger's boots.

"What are you doing?" demanded Mr. Roger truculently.

"We will help you dress," explained Rainbird.

"Don't need to dress. Am dressed. Oh, my aching head." Mr. Roger lurched across the room and was sick in the fireplace. Joseph turned green and clutched his heaving stomach.

"Are you ready, Jolly Roger?" came Lord Guy's cheerful voice.

Mr. Roger rallied amazingly. "Coming," he roared.

"Feeling better?" called his lordship.

"Lots. I just cascaded in the fireplace."

"That's the ticket. Come along."

Rainbird and Joseph mutely followed Mr. Roger out. On the first landing, Lord Guy was waiting with an amused smile on his rakish face. He was dressed in impeccable evening clothes—black coat, fawn silk breeches, and pumps —and he carried a flat bicorne under his arm.

He raised his quizzing glass and surveyed Mr. Roger. "Demne," he said, "here comes the wreck of the regiment."

"Shall you wish to dine later, my lord?" asked Rainbird.

"Think we'll eat somewhere outside," said Lord Guy.

He linked arms with Mr. Roger, and the pair of them went down the stairs and out the front door into the street.

It took Jenny an hour with Alice's help to clean Lord Guy's bedroom, which was a mess of discarded clothes, wet towels, and empty glasses, while Rainbird and Joseph drew off the water in cans and carried the bath downstairs. Rainbird remarked gloomily the water was as clean as it had been when they had filled the bath, which all went to show my lord was going to be an eccentric washer.

"The newspapers say his commander-in-chief has a cold bath every morning," he said.

Joseph let out an alarmed squawk. "What! Cerry thet beth up them stairs every day!"

"Maybe he'll go to the hummums," said Rainbird, meaning the Turkish baths in Jermyn Street.

"Eh hope he falls in and gets drownded," said Joseph pettishly. "Where's that servant of his? He should have cleaned some of that mess."

"Gone with his master."

"Good riddance."

Meanwhile, the two friends, shadowed by Manuel, set

out to carouse at every well-known establishment in town from the hells of Jermyn Street to the Royal Saloon in Piccadilly, shopping for females as they went. Every time Lord Guy or Mr. Roger saw a particularly pretty female of the Fashionable Impure, they handed over cards and solemnly invited her to a party at 67 Clarges Street the following night. After sampling some of the wares, they settled down to a night of heavy drinking and gambling and ended up reeling through Berkeley Square as a red sun rose over frosty London. The weather had turned cold again.

Mr. Roger keeled over in the grass in the middle of Berkeley Square and fell asleep. Lord Guy, feeling tired and jaded, called over his shoulder for Manuel to go back to the mews and fetch the carriage to take Mr. Roger home.

Lord Guy was strolling past the houses on the west side of the square, when, through an open doorway, he saw a lady standing at the top of the staircase inside the house.

She was in her undress. She wore a flowing nightgown and a pretty negligee. She had glorious red hair brushed down on her shoulders. There was an oil lamp on a table on the landing where she stood, and it illuminated her calm face and splendid Junoesque figure. The butler, who had left the door open while he got a breath of air, was on the other side of the square and did not notice Lord Guy.

Lord Guy walked straight into the house and up the stairs. "You, madam," he said in an awed voice, "are the most beautiful thing I have ever seen."

Her eyes, he noticed dreamily, were a peculiar mixture of blue and green and gold. He had never seen eyes like these before. Very drunk and walking in a dream-world, Lord Guy advanced on the goddess, holding out his arms.

She never said a word. She raised one beautifully arched foot in its beaded slipper and kicked out with all her force. The blow caught him right at the waistline. He tumbled backwards, down the stairs.

As he was very drunk, he had not tensed any of his muscles, and so, when he sat up at the foot of the stairs, he was unhurt.

From a long way off, he could hear bells ringing and feet running. Before the lady's servants picked him up to throw him out, he caught a glimpse of himself in a long looking-glass in the hall.

At first he did not recognise the dissipated drunk who stared back at him. When he did, the shock was so great, he let the servants bundle him out into the street without a murmur of protest.

He reeled home and fell headlong into bed without removing his clothes.

Rainbird, hearing Mr. Roger return, roused Joseph and said wearily they might as well see if they could be of any help. They dressed slowly, neither of them anxious to face their master so soon. When they looked into Mr. Roger's room, he was already sleeping peacefully, having been undressed by Manuel.

They went down another floor and walked into Lord Guy's room and stopped short on the threshold. The door had been open, so the Spaniard had not heard them coming. He was standing by the bed, looking down at his master, his face twisted into a mask of hate.

"Can we help you?" asked Rainbird.

Manuel's face once more resumed its smooth, supercilious expression.

"No, I thank you," he said disdainfully. "Close the door behind you when you go."

Chapter
Two

When I loved you, I can't but allow
I had many an exquisite minute;
But the scorn that I feel for you now
Hath even more luxury in it.

Thus, whether we're on or we're off,
Some witchery seems to await you;
To love you was pleasant enough,
And, oh! 'tis delicious to hate you!

—THOMAS MOORE

It was a typical spring day—that is, a wind all the way from Siberia was cutting around the buildings and sooty flakes of snow were beginning to cover the ground.

Miss Esther Jones of 120 Berkeley Square shivered as she looked out of the window. It would be much too cold to take the children walking.

She brushed her rich red tresses and wound them into a severe knot on the top of her head, rather like a doorknob. Only fools wore muslin or silk in such weather, according to the sensible Miss Jones, so she put on a warm wool gown of a depressing mud-coloured hue.

She wondered idly who that drunk man had been who had walked so calmly into her home, and then dismissed the matter from her mind. London was full of crass drunks. One learned quickly how to deal with them—and with careless butlers who strolled out and left the door open.

By the time she had finished dressing, Miss Jones looked more like a governess than the very rich lady she actually was.

But circumstances had done much to change her from the carefree girl she had once been. Her father, Squire Hugh Jones, had led a disgraceful sort of life at his country home, causing all sorts of scandals in the neighbourhood before falling into an apoplexy and departing this world. His timid and ailing wife, Miss Jones' mother, had survived him by only one year. That had left Miss Jones his sole heir. It also left her in charge of her young brother, nine-year-old Peter, and his twin sister Amy, the late Mrs. Jones having been blessed with two more children when she least expected to have any.

Esther Jones had found herself very rich indeed. The squire had been a successful gambler on 'Change, and the fortune he left turned out to be immense.

Esther now detested the country and country people. She thought the country was undisciplined and disorderly, all those messy trees and flowers. She had bought the mansion in Berkeley Square, packed up, and moved to Town. She had taken over the education of the twins herself. She had first taken herself in hand, ruthlessly eradicating all her father's character defects she might have inherited—bar one, if it could be called a defect. Esther had taken over her father's speculations where he had left off and had proceeded to make herself into one of the richest women in England.

Since she did not cultivate the friendship of society or aspire to rise to the aristocracy, little was known about her and nobody came to call.

The house was richly furnished. From Pembroke table to sabre-legged chair, everything glowed and shone. Everything was also rather dark and gloomy. Light colours dirtied easily, so the curtains and bed hangings and carpets were all of a serviceable dark red colour.

She not only instructed her little brother and sister, but her servants as well. They were expected to assemble in the drawing room every morning for prayers, and then at various appointed times during the week to attend classes. The men were taught reading, writing, and arithmetic, and the women, fine sewing, reading, and how to keep household accounts.

She paid good wages but found it strangely hard to keep servants. She did not know they were bored to death and longed for employment in a more free and easy establishment.

As a young girl—Esther was now twenty-six—she had been shamed and embarrassed by her father's drunken behaviour. Day after day, she worked to make sure those days were gone forever and that everyone surrounding her remained staid and respectable.

She was glad the weather was bad because sunshine would have meant the children would have pressed her to take them to one of the parks, and parks reminded Esther of the country. Also, there were soldiers drilling in the parks and she thought young Peter was much too fascinated with uniforms and guns for his own good. Peter was being brought up to be fit to take over the business reins when he reached twenty-one. Esther detested all army men, damning them as uncouth louts, although she was not alone in this. The British had always detested their army and it seemed they always would. Quite a number of taverns had signs posted outside saying "No redcoats."

As usual, she conducted prayers, ate a hearty breakfast, read a chapter of the Bible to the twins, and then prepared to take them upstairs to the schoolroom for their lessons.

It was then that Peter noticed the snow had stopped and pale sunlight was flooding the square outside.

"Do take us out, Esther," he begged. "We are always inside. It is so *stuffy.*"

"No, it is very cold," said Esther. "You will catch an inflammation."

"If we do not get fresh air," said little Amy primly, "mayhap we will both go into a decline. Peter is very white."

Esther bit her lip in vexation. Amy bowed her red head and meekly studied her hands. She was beginning to learn how to manipulate her elder sister.

Peter did *look white,* thought Esther with a pang. There were blue shadows under his eyes.

"Very well," she said reluctantly. "Tell John to attend us." John was the first footman.

The children scampered upstairs to get dressed. "You'd better scrub that blanc off your face, Peter," said Amy. "If you keep it on, she'll notice it when we get outside into the daylight."

"Righto!" said Peter, scrubbing his face and leaving smears of blanc on the towel. "Good idea of yours, Amy."

Esther had to admit to herself as they walked through Hyde Park and into Kensington Gardens that she was glad they had decided to go out. The snow was melting rapidly, the sun was warm, and there was a feeling of anticipation in the air. Her hair, screwed up under a repellent hat like a coal-scuttle, felt heavy and uncomfortable. Two young misses and their mother passed in a carriage. The girls were wearing little straw hats. Underneath, their hair had been cut in one of the latest crops.

How sensible, thought the old Esther wistfully. *Fustian,* the new stern Esther told herself. *Only see how everyone is staring at them. I have had enough of vulgar curiosity in my life.*

She sat down on an iron bench and arranged her skirts and took a book out of her reticule, which was an enormous dull red brocade affair made out of left-over upholstery material, because, Esther believed, economies must be practised no matter how rich one was. Mortification was good for the soul.

"I will now read to you," said Esther. Peter emitted something very much like a groan. Esther looked at him sharply, but he smiled sweetly back at her, showing his dimples.

The footman wandered off and stood watching the troops.

Esther cleared her throat and began to read. "This poem is entitled 'The School,'" she said. Peter sat up and paid attention. He longed to go to school and play with other boys.

"There was a little girl so proud,
She talked so fast and laughed so loud,
That those who came with her to play
Were always glad to go away.
In bracelets, necklace she did shine;
Her clothes were always very fine.
Her frocks through carelessness were soiled;
In truth she was already spoiled.
Her mother died; she went to school,

And there obliged to live by rule,
Though oft before the time for bed,
A cap and bells disgraced her head."

Peter's attention began to wander. He twisted round. There was a little servant girl standing behind the bench on which they were sitting, listening to Esther's reading.

"When false indulgence warps the mind,
The discipline of school we find
Most efficacious to correct
The ills arising from neglect.

"Now what did you think of *that?*" asked Esther brightly.

"It's about girls," said Peter, "and girls have an awful time at school anyway. Boys don't."

"You are a very lucky little boy," said Esther severely. "You would find school quite horrible and you would be tormented by great louts of boys. Listen, I shall read you the story of little Henry. *That* is about a boy."

She fished in her capacious reticule and brought out another book entitled *A Cup of Sweets that can never Cloy; or Delightful Tales for Good Children,* by a London Lady, and began to read.

Even Esther began to think the tale of little Henry was quite depressing. He was a boy who insisted on having his own way the whole time. When he was told, say, not to jump down three stairs at a time or he might hurt himself, he always replied angrily that he was a not a baby and knew how to take care of himself.

One day, an aunt gave Henry a seven-shilling piece. But instead of consulting his dear parents and asking them what to do with it, he bought a large quantity of gunpowder, blew up the nursery, lost an eye, killed his little sister, but was a very good boy from that day forth.

"I should think he would be," said Amy, putting her hands over her mouth to stifle a giggle.

"That girl's listening to you," said Peter, pointing to the servant girl behind the seat.

The girl made to move away, but Esther smiled at her and said, "Come here. You may listen to me read, if you wish."

"I can read myself, ma'am," said the girl proudly.

"Indeed! What is your name?"

"Lizzie O'Brien, ma'am."

"And where do you work?"

"Sixty-seven Clarges Street, an' it please you, ma'am. I'm a scullery maid."

"I am Miss Jones . . . my brother and sister, Master Peter and Miss Amy. Who taught you to read, Lizzie?"

"Our butler set up a school in the servants' hall, but it's the Scotch cook what teaches us."

"*Who* teaches us," corrected Esther. "This is amazing. I, too, teach my servants, but they do not thank me for my pains. I would like to speak to this butler of yours."

"Mr. Rainbird, ma'am."

Esther fished out a card. "Be so good as to tell Mr. Rainbird to call on me during his free time. I am nearly always at home."

Lizzie, who had come round the front of the bench, took the card and dropped a curtsy. She turned to go away and then stopped in surprise.

"What is it?" asked Esther.

"It's that little man over there," said Lizzie. "He's that foreign servant what 'as just come to stay."

Esther looked across the park. A sallow, foreign-looking servant in pink-and-black livery was standing under a tree, writing busily in a notebook.

"He's watching the troops!" cried Peter, jumping up and down. "He might be a French spy."

"He's Spanish," said Lizzie.

"Besides," said Esther, "he only has to read the newspapers, which give the exact numbers of the volunteers."

"Maybe he didn't think of that," said Peter.

Esther turned her attention to Lizzie. *Such a pleasant clean girl,* she thought. "Goodbye, Miss O'Brien," she said.

Lizzie flushed to the roots of her hair with pleasure at the great compliment. Very few of her fellow servants could even remember her second name.

Esther was immensely reassured by the meeting. At 67 Clarges Street was a house where the desire for cleanliness and education was as great as in her own. But this Rainbird appeared to have willing pupils. She was anxious to find out how he had managed to achieve it.

Lizzie came bursting into the servants' hall to tell them all her news. Rainbird was intrigued with the idea of making a social call on a lady in Berkeley Square, but the others were inclined to think Miss Jones one of those nosey, interfering reformers. Disappointed by the reception of her story, she forgot to tell them about Manuel.

It was three in the afternoon. Lord Guy and Mr. Roger were still asleep, and Manuel had not put in an appearance, when the servants received a visitor.

There was the sound of a silk skirt swishing down the area steps and then a rap at the kitchen door.

"It's probably Lizzie's reformer," said Mrs. Middleton. "Let us pretend there's no one at home."

"She might go up and knock at the street door and wake my lord," said Rainbird, going to the door.

An extremely fat little lady stood on the step. She was dressed in a brown silk gown covered with a sealskin coat. Her face was very plump, and her eyes were almost buried in pads of fat.

She twinkled up at the butler. "John, my love," she said with a charming laugh. "Don't you recognise me?"

Rainbird's heart did a somersault. He knew that voice and that laugh. They both belonged to Felice, the lady's maid who had broken his heart and gone to Brighton to get married. He looked wildly around, suspecting some trick, and expecting Felice to come dancing out from behind this matron's fat back.

"It is I. *C'est moi!* Felice."

"Come in, Felice," said Rainbird, backing away before her.

While the others exclaimed and asked questions, Rainbird covertly studied the love of his life. He could not believe it was Felice. He closed his eyes, hearing her voice, willing this little fat lady to go away and leave the real Felice in her place. But when he opened his eyes, she was still there, laughing and preening and showing off her fur coat to Mrs. Middleton. "And she used to be so silent," he marvelled.

She talked on and on about how good her husband was. Her Jack was an alderman and doing nicely, thank you. She had picked up a great number of common English expressions, and her voice had coarsened.

She rattled on non-stop for about an hour. Then she said teasingly to Rainbird, "My, but you're the quiet one, John." She turned to the others and giggled. "Our John was quite spoony about me at one time, wasn't you, *mon cher?*"

Rainbird gritted his teeth. He *hated* her. He had loved

her with a fine and noble passion, a passion this horrible dumpy woman was coyly describing as "spoony."

Manuel came into the servants' hall and said curtly, "Hock and seltzer for my lord."

"Get it yourself," said Rainbird.

Felice looked sharply at Manuel and spoke to him in rapid French. He looked back at her, his face impassive.

"He isn't French," said Joseph. "He's Spanish."

Felice raised her eyebrows but did not say any more. She kissed Rainbird, who flinched, on the cheek, and departed in a rustle of silk, leaving a cloud of musky perfume behind her.

They all bustled about, avoiding Rainbird, feeling sorry for him. Only Mrs. Middleton was glad. She still nursed a *tendre* for the butler. She had been hurt and had wept into her pillow when he had fallen in love with that woman. Now Rainbird had seen Felice in her true colours. It was awful what fat could do to a woman, thought Mrs. Middleton, resolving then and there to buy herself a new corset come quarter-day.

After a few hours of looking at the shops, Felice settled herself inside the Brighton coach with the comfortable feeling of a job well done. She enjoyed being plump, and her doting husband called her "a cosy armful." But she had often thought of John Rainbird, and, although her practical French soul considered undying love without money a waste of time, her conscience had at last prompted her to do her best to throw cold water on Rainbird's passion.

With the vulgar personality she had briefly assumed left behind her in Clarges Street, she looked like a quiet and charming, if fat, lady.

The coach rattled out over the cobbles. Felice remembered that odd servant, Manuel. She was sure he was

French. But what happened at Number 67 Clarges Street was no longer her concern.

Lord Guy sat wrapped in a silk dressing gown and sipped his hock and seltzer. He tried to remember what he had been up to the night before, but it only came back to him in highly coloured flashes. He frowned. Something very important had happened to him, and for the life of him he could not remember what it was.

Mr. Roger slouched in, wearing only his night-shirt and nightcap.

"You look like a sick gorilla," said Lord Guy pleasantly. "Sit down and have some hock and seltzer."

"I'd better," said Mr. Roger gloomily. "Got to restore my energies for this affair tonight." He grinned and winked. "Or should I say 'affairs.'"

"Are we going somewhere?" asked Lord Guy.

"No, somewhere's coming here. Don't you remember, we invited that party of bloods and a crowd of the best-looking high-fliers to come *here.*"

Lord Guy closed his eyes. He had a sudden longing for a quiet evening alone with a book.

But he had escaped death so many times. After the Season, it would be back to shattered bones, dysentery, and cannon fire.

"Then we had better warn our prim servants," he said. "Manuel!"

The Spanish servant appeared from behind a screen. "Send that housekeeper to me, and Rainbird as well."

Rainbird and Mrs. Middleton listened carefully to his instructions. A supper for about fifty was to be served at two in the morning. Musicians were to be sent for. Champagne was to be got in by the crate and ice by the bucket.

Mrs. Middleton blenched. "My lord," she said timidly, "how are we to seat fifty?"

Lord Guy frowned. Then his face cleared. "You'll need to clear this place out, that is, the hall, the front and back parlours, this bedroom of mine—I'll move upstairs—and the dining room. Put in tables up here and let them stand about and help themselves. Chalk the floors downstairs and put the orchestra in the back parlour."

Rainbird consoled himself with the thought that fifty members of the ton would make good pickings for the Vail Box.

"What about decoration, my lord?" he asked.

Lord Guy looked blank.

"I mean," pursued Rainbird, "there is usually some theme at a supper party—eastern or sylvan or . . ."

"Don't matter," said Lord Guy. "The ladies will supply ample decoration."

"There is the matter of wages, my lord," said Rainbird tentatively.

"Aren't you paid any?"

"Yes, my lord, very low wages when the house is empty. It is the custom for a tenant to pay the difference during the Season—that is, raise the servants' wages to a normal level."

Lord Guy shrugged. "Sounds like a hum to me," he said indifferently. "But I am causing you a great deal of work. Pay yourselves what you think fit and present me with the bill."

The servants were at first appalled by the amount of last-minute work facing them, for the guests were to begin to arrive around eight in the evening. But the news that an increase in their wages had been agreed on made them all work cheerfully and hard.

Angus MacGregor was a chef who enjoyed drama. The

son of an earl would entertain only the cream of society. The cook planned to amaze and delight.

The first shock came around eight-thirty when the staid environs of Clarges Street were enlivened by the arrival of an open carriage brim-full of London's Fashionable Impure.

They were painted and feathered and beribboned. Despite the chill of the evening, they were dressed in transparent muslin gowns, cut short in some cases to reveal glimpses of ankle, and, in others, pinned up on either side to expose legs encased in flesh-coloured tights.

Rainbird tried to bar the door, thinking they were all looking for a fashionable brothel, but they triumphantly produced cards, and Mr. Roger appeared on the scene to welcome them.

Another carriage full of demi-reps rolled up, followed by carriages driven by bucks and bloods, Choice Spirits, Pinks of the Ton, and Corinthians.

Rainbird, his face set in a mask of disapproval, went downstairs to tell all the women servants to stay where they were and on no account to venture upstairs. Dave was crammed into a makeshift sort of page's livery and put on duty. Angus was beside himself with rage to think he had wasted his art to feed a parcel of doxies.

At first it seemed reassuringly like any other supper party. They danced, they chatted, they played cards. But bottle after bottle of champagne began to disappear and then the ladies called for rum.

Then they played Hunt the Slipper, an innocuous-enough game, but the ladies ran about screaming, and some of them began to complain about the heat and took off their dresses.

Dave was sent downstairs.

When suppertime came, Joseph trembled and averted

his eyes as he handed out plates of food to near-naked guests. The only one still formally attired was Lord Guy, but he was very drunk and seemed to be highly diverted by the goings-on.

Joseph found himself thinking about Lizzie and about how he had snubbed her of late. *Lizzie was good,* he thought, longing for the maid's quiet reassurance. He resolved to slip out on the morrow and buy her a little present.

One young lady with enormous bosoms had rested them on a plate and was offering them to Lord Guy. Lord Guy waved his quizzing glass and said languidly they looked a trifle underdone.

Everyone laughed, and Joseph's delicate stomach heaved. *I'll never have another erotic dream again,* he thought, unaware that Rainbird was thinking the same thing.

All that female flesh, Rainbird was wondering, *it's funny how it puts you off the idea.*

At last supper was over and Rainbird and Joseph were told they might retire to bed. Manuel stayed where he was, standing behind his master's chair.

"Best get some sleep," muttered Rainbird to Joseph. "This place is going to be like a sty in the morning."

Miss Esther Jones awoke early to a fine day. She felt restless and decided to go for a walk before summoning the servants to morning prayers.

She remembered that little scullery maid, Lizzie, with pleasure, and her steps took her towards Clarges Street.

At first she thought there was a fire at Number 67. Servants from the other houses were standing out on the street, gazing up at the windows.

She quickened her pace and joined the audience.

One man gave a coarse laugh and pointed upwards. The house was still a blaze of lights. At a first-floor window there appeared to be a huge fat man's face pressed against the glass. The crowd began to laugh and cheer, and with flaming cheeks Miss Esther Jones realized she was looking at a bare female bottom on which someone had painted a grinning face.

As she watched, thunderstruck, a man lifted the naked woman away from the window and looked down. He was fully dressed in evening clothes. He had a rakish, handsome face, golden hair, and bright blue eyes. Esther recognised the drunk who had walked so boldly into her house.

He looked at the watching crowd in an amused way and then his eyes alighted on Esther and sharpened. He turned away from the window, and Esther knew he was going to come down and speak to her.

She turned and ran off down the street as fast as she could and did not stop until she was safely inside her home in Berkeley Square and had locked the door behind her.

Chapter
Three

Pious Selinda goes to prayers,
If I but ask her favour;
And yet the silly fool's in tears,
If she believes I'll leave her,
Would I were free from this restraint,
Or else had hopes to win her;
Would she make of me a saint,
Or I of her a sinner.

—WILLIAM CONGREVE

By noon the morning after the supper party, the servants rolled up their sleeves and grimly got to work. Angus MacGregor had to be summoned from the kitchen to help decant the bodies out into the street. Half-dressed men and women cursed him roundly, but he swore at them in Gaelic and brandished his meat cleaver, and soon the house appeared to be clear of guests.

Then there was the disgusting mess of brimming chamber-pots, filthy floors, remains of food, and broken glass to be cleared.

Manuel had disappeared again. He was not in the attic

room he shared with MacGregor, nor was he downstairs.

"Probably sleeping at the end of his master's bed like a bleeding dawg," muttered Joseph, who had lost his refined accents during all the work. He picked up a soiled garter from under the dining table and threw it on the fire. It was a good thing Lizzie was busy at the sink washing dishes and glasses, thought Joseph. The leavings of the guests were enough to corrupt any young girl's mind. He thought again about getting Lizzie a present. But the shops would surely be closed by the time they had finished their work.

By four in the afternoon, Jenny called Lizzie from her dishes and asked her to help in the gentlemen's bedrooms. It was time to clear the fires and take up cans of hot water. They would surely soon be awake and getting dressed, ready for another wild evening.

Carrying a large bucket of coal, Lizzie struggled up the stairs after Jenny.

"We'll start off with his lordship's room," said Jenny, opening the door.

She and Lizzie stood thunderstruck in the doorway. His lordship was in bed with three naked females who lay draped about him like rumpled white blankets.

Lord Guy awoke, struggled up against the pillows, and stared at the two maids who stood there goggling, their faces crimson. He looked at his bed companions and frowned. *Had he actually* had *any of them?* he wondered vaguely. Then he looked at Lizzie's innocent shocked face, and said curtly, "Get out! I shall send for you when the room is empty."

Jenny dragged Lizzie back and slammed the door.

Lord Guy kicked one naked body out of bed and then another. The demi-reps screamed and groaned. He promised the highest payment to the one who dressed and left first. There was an undignified scramble, but it speeded them on their way.

He rang the bell. Rainbird answered it wearing his working clothes and apron. He stood to attention, his eyes lowered and his whole acrobat's body bristling with outrage.

"Bring me a bath," Lord Guy ordered.

Rainbird briefly raised his eyes and then lowered them. "Certainly, my lord," he said.

"Wait a minute," said Lord Guy. "There was an insolent look in your eye there, fellow. What is the meaning of it?"

"The maids in this house, including Mrs. Middleton, are in my charge," said Rainbird. "I am protective of them, perhaps too much. I gather the scullery maid and the chambermaid were deeply shocked. I know such behaviour goes on in society, my lord, but usually it is . . ."

He broke off.

"Usually it is confined to the brothels," said Lord Guy. "Are you always so cheeky to your masters, Rainbird?"

"No, my lord. I apologise. I did not mean to let my disapproval show."

"Don't let it show again. Your station does not prevent you from a horsewhipping. Now get that bath!"

Rainbird bowed and left.

Lord Guy rolled over in bed. He felt a lump and brought out an empty rum bottle.

He sat up and clutched his head. Then he looked about the room. What a squalid mess! No wonder that butler had been disapproving. He rang the bell again and demanded Manuel's presence. Rainbird was about to say he did not know where Manuel was when the Spaniard appeared behind him, making him jump.

"Clean up this mess, Manuel."

The servant turned a cold eye on Rainbird. "Where are the maids?" he demanded.

Lord Guy's voice was like silk. "I told you to clean it up," he said. "Hop to it!"

He swung his long legs out of bed and shrugged his dressing gown over his naked body. "You," he said to Rainbird, "come with me."

He led the way down to the dining room. Alice and Jenny were sprinkling rose water over the carpet. They started and blushed when they saw him and then stood with lowered eyes.

What a monster these creatures make me feel, thought Lord Guy irritably.

"Out," he said aloud, jerking his head at the door.

When they had left, he turned and surveyed Rainbird. "Well, my Methodist friend," he said, "out with it. Was there more to shock the females than my companions?"

"Yes, my lord," said Rainbird stoutly, although he could already feel his shoulders smart under a horsewhipping. With averted eyes, he described in detail the state of the house and of the remaining guests.

Lord Guy felt his spirits sink to his naked feet. Where was all the happy-go-lucky bachelor freedom he had imagined?

He had been brought up to treat servants well. The men in his regiment had never had cause to complain of his treatment. These servants were as much under his command as his soldiers, and he had let them down.

"You will not be troubled again," he said stiffly. "Mr. Roger and I shall take our pleasures elsewhere. You may pay the staff two pounds each for their trouble."

"Thank you, my lord," gasped Rainbird.

"Hard being in service, is it not?" went on Lord Guy, looking at the butler curiously.

"It can be, my lord, but there are compensations."

"Such as receiving extra payment from guilty masters?"

"Not quite, my lord," said Rainbird, risking a smile. "We, the servants here, are become much attached to each other. It is not often a man is blessed with such a good family."

Lord Guy frowned, and Rainbird wondered whether he had said something wrong. But Lord Guy was remembering his own family in Yorkshire. He should really visit his mother and father before returning to the wars.

Was his planned celebration in London to burn out so soon? To lead a quieter life would bring the memories of the hell of war rushing back into his brain, to hear again the cannon's roar and hear the shrieks of the wounded and smell the putrid flesh of the dead and dying. He turned very pale and swayed slightly.

"My lord?" Rainbird made a step forward to catch his master should he fall.

"I shall do very well," said Lord Guy. "Bring me a bottle of canary and tell the Jolly Roger to make himself ready."

He smiled at the butler, a charming, devastating smile.

"Well, well," said Rainbird, shaking his head as he made his way down the stairs.

He said nothing to the others for the moment. He and Joseph and the girls carried the bath and the cans of hot water upstairs. Mr. Roger's bed turned out to be free of visitors. He revived himself by pouring two cans of water over his head and shaking himself like a dog.

At last both gentlemen, shadowed by Manuel, made their way out.

The staff of Number 67 heaved a sigh of relief. "I don't know as I can take much more o' this," said Joseph.

"He's given us two pounds each for our pains," said Rainbird.

Everyone brightened. "It is a pity my lord is so evil," said Lizzie.

"I think he's a good man," said Rainbird. "He's been at the wars too long. He said there would be no repetition of last night, and what's more, I believe him."

"He's ever so handsome," said Alice dreamily.

"He frightens *me,*" said Jenny stoutly. "I never hope to see such a disgusting sight again."

Mrs. Middleton was disposed to be kind. She was still floating along on a wave of euphoria caused by the comeuppance of Felice. "What he needs," she said, "is the love of a good woman."

"A good woman," jeered Dave. "He's 'ad free o' them at onct."

"Don't talk dirty," said Jenny.

"I mean it," pursued Mrs. Middleton. "They always reform when they meet a good woman."

Rainbird shrugged. "Only in books," he said.

Lord Guy and Mr. Roger returned home at three in the morning, a comparatively early hour. They asked to be awakened at nine as they planned to join a Four-in-Hand-Club expedition to Box Hill. They did not expect to be back until the day after that. The servants might do as they pleased.

With great courage, Rainbird presented Lord Guy at breakfast with the bill for the increased wages plus the bonus of two pounds a head.

Lord Guy paid out the bonus and wrote a draft to his bank for the wages without a murmur.

He was surprised to find the whole staff lined up in the

hall to say goodbye to him, with Rainbird as their spokes-man to thank him on behalf of them all for the money.

He gave a slight bow and gave them a mocking smile. "Don't spend it all on riotous living," he said. He made a graceful exit, with Mr. Roger lumbering like a bear after him.

"He's awfully nice when he smiles," said Alice senti-mentally.

They all crowded back down to the servants' hall to decide what to do with their day of freedom. Lizzie, who liked to walk in the parks and get as much fresh air as she could, said she would probably go to Kensington Gardens. Joseph coughed genteelly and said he would accompany her, and Lizzie blushed with pleasure.

Angus said he would look at the second-hand book-stalls, and Jenny and Alice wanted to see the shops. Mrs. Middleton looked hopefully at Rainbird, but he said he would go round to Berkeley Square to call on "Lizzie's reformer." He said that after that he would go to my lord's bank, bring back the wages and put half the money in the Vail Box, which was where they kept their savings towards buying their pub. Then he gave them two pounds each. Mrs. Middleton volunteered to stay to look after the house. She meant to be ready and available for any outing when Rainbird returned from the bank.

Rainbird did not expect this Miss Jones to be up and about at such an early hour, but he thought he would call and arrange a suitable time.

It was a cold, sunny morning. As he strolled round to Berkeley Square, Rainbird thought with amusement of Mrs. Middleton's idea of reforming Lord Guy.

Miss Esther Jones' butler stared at Rainbird's livery and gave him a mournful look. "Come to take my job, have you?" he said.

"No," said Rainbird. "Miss Jones wishes to see me to discuss the matter of servants' education. I have no intention of changing my employ, and Miss Jones has no intention of suggesting such a thing. I realise it is too early in the day to expect Miss Jones to be awake, but I hoped to make a firm appointment for the afternoon."

"It's never too early for madam," said the butler gloomily. "Up at six most mornings. What's the protocol for servants visiting quality? Very strict on protocol is Miss Jones."

"You leave me in the hall," said Rainbird, "and then she'll take me into whichever room she thinks fit."

"Thanks," said the moody butler. "Got a card?"

Rainbird passed one over. "Bring it back," he said. "It's the only one I've got."

He stood in the hall after the butler had mounted the stairs and looked about him. Everything was very rich, very polished, and very gloomy. From abovestairs came the piping sound of children's voices raised in a hymn. Rainbird began to wish he had not come. There was something claustrophobic about the mansion. Rainbird thought of Lord Guy's supper party. "Out of hell into heaven," he said to himself, "and I'm comfortable neither place."

There was a light step on the stairs, and Rainbird looked up.

He thought he had never seen a more magnificent creature. She was very tall and deep-bosomed. Her hair was scraped up under an unflattering cap, but it could not take away from the perfection of her figure, the creaminess of her skin, or the strange beauty of her large eyes.

He thought she must be Miss Jones' niece, but she advanced on him with a smile and said, "I am Miss Jones. You, I presume, are Rainbird. Follow me."

She led the way into a saloon on the ground floor. It

was very dark, and tall dark pieces of furniture stood about like so many disapproving members of the clergy.

"Sit down," said Esther.

Rainbird sat down on a hard, overstuffed chair, and Esther sat down opposite him and regarded him gravely.

"I must begin by saying I was in two minds as to whether to give you an audience or not," she said. "As you have heard, I was much impressed by the education and cleanliness of your scullery maid. But," she went on, a slight blush rising to her cheeks, "I had occasion to pass Sixty-seven Clarges Street early yesterday morning. There was a Bacchanalia in progress."

"That was a supper party given by our new tenant, Lord Guy Carlton," said Rainbird. "The morals of the masters are not necessarily those of the servants, particularly in a house which is only rented out for the Season."

"I am glad to hear it," said Esther severely. "This Lord Guy must be a disgusting and licentious rake."

"He has been at the wars a long time, I gather," said Rainbird cautiously. "I do not think it my place to discuss my master, but I should like to point out that I do not think there will be a recurrence of the scenes you witnessed. His lordship was good enough to say he would in future take his pleasures elsewhere."

"At least that shows *some* conscience," said Esther. "Now, I am interested in the fact that you hold a school for the staff. I give my servants lessons every day, but they are slow at their books, and surly, and unwilling to learn. Have you come across the same problem?"

"No, ma'am. It came about spontaneously. One of the previous tenants took it upon herself to educate Lizzie. The education fever spread to the rest of us. We decided to pass the winter months in study. Our cook, Angus MacGregor, is Scotch, and it was he, in fact, who led the classes. You see, ma'am, if any of them did not want to be bothered with studies, they only had to say so. Angus turned out to be a good teacher. He said if people were encouraged to read exciting stories, then enjoyment of reading led to higher things. To that end, he bought romances for the ladies, and sporting magazines for the men."

"But romances!" said Esther, shocked.

"They are quite moral," said Rainbird seriously, "and very amusing. The villain always pays for his crimes, and the heroine is always pure and innocent. It's a sort of way of instilling morals enjoyably—like giving children pleasant-tasting medicine."

"This is fascinating," said Esther, her fine eyes glowing. "May I offer you tea, Rainbird?"

Rainbird accepted. As Esther talked about the difficulties of education, he studied her covertly. Here, surely, was Mrs. Middleton's good woman. She appeared very strict in her ways, and yet she had a charming easiness of manner, not at all high in the instep. There were few members of the ton in Berkeley Square, reflected Rainbird, who would dream of entertaining a butler to tea.

As the conversation moved to more general topics, Rainbird became aware that Miss Jones did not appear to go about socially. She must be encouraged. Mrs. Middleton's idea, which had seemed so foolish, now seemed quite reasonable. It was important to get Lord Guy and Miss Jones together, and the way to do that would be to encourage Miss Jones to attend the opera or a few routs.

"You must have social ambitions for your little sister," he ventured after a lull in the conversation.

Esther laughed. "Her début is a long way away."

"But you naturally hope she will marry well," pursued Rainbird, "and you are in an excellent position to begin to make friends among the ton who will be useful to both children when they grow up."

Esther frowned. She had never thought of the twins' growing up and marrying. But this odd butler had a point.

"Besides," said Rainbird, "I am sure they would like friends to play with. It is very important for children to have friends."

"They have each other," said Esther defensively.

Rainbird, feeling he had almost gone too far, turned the conversation back to education, and the visit ended on a pleasant note.

After he had left, Esther sat a long time deep in thought. She had never before thought of education as being fun. *Children* were *supposed to have fun,* she thought with a guilty pang. London was full of theatres and circuses and menageries.

At last she roused herself. She would go out to Hatchard's bookshop in Piccadilly and buy some entertaining books for the children and for the staff.

Beguiled by the bright sunshine outside the windows, she set out wearing insufficient clothing. By the time she set out to walk back from Piccadilly, an icy wind was blowing and a thin sleety rain whipped against her clothes.

By the next morning, she had a raging cold. Wearily, she summoned the twins and told them they must make shift to look after themselves until she felt better.

"What shall we do, Peter?" asked Amy when they were back in the nursery.

Peter's eyes shone. "Why don't we slip out on our own and go to Kensington Gardens?"

"That's not much fun. Why there?"

"To look for that French spy. We could follow him and unmask him and get a medal from the king!"

"Oooh," breathed Amy. "Let's go."

The afternoon was dry but steely grey with a biting wind. The twins told their nursery maid that they were going to play quietly by themselves, and, when she had gone off, they put on their coats and slipped quietly out of the house.

Hand in hand, they trotted quickly through Hyde Park and into Kensington Gardens.

They searched and searched for an hour until they were tired out.

"We'd best be getting back," said Peter, disappointed.

He took Amy's hand and they set off home. But as they left Kensington Gardens and entered Hyde Park, Peter stiffened and clutched Amy.

"Look!" he said. "Over there."

The Bloomsbury Volunteers were drilling on an open patch of ground. Standing watching them and making notes in a small black book was Manuel.

"What do we do?" asked Amy, her voice squeaky with excitement.

"We creep stealthily up on him and try to see what he's writing," said Peter. "Come on!"

They crept up behind Manuel until they were almost next to him. Peter raised himself on his tiptoes to see if he could make out what the servant was writing in his book. At the same moment, Amy let out a tremendous sneeze. Manuel looked quickly over his shoulder and saw the small boy, obviously trying to read what he had written.

He seized them both by the arms and started to shake them. "What you look at me for, heh?" he shouted.

"We weren't doing anything," gasped Peter bravely, but Amy, thoroughly terrified, began to scream.

"Manuel! Leave those children alone this minute!" came a loud voice.

Manuel's sallow face flushed, and he dropped the children's arms. Peter and Amy clutched each other and stared up at their rescuer. He was tall and fair and dressed elegantly.

"My lord," said Manuel sulkily, "these brats, they sneak up on me and frighten me."

"What! A couple of small children! You must do better than that."

"He's a spy!" cried Peter. "He's watching the troops and writing in his book."

"He does not need to count the troops when anyone can read all the details in the newspapers," said Lord Guy. "But let me see this book, Manuel."

Manuel produced a small black book. Lord Guy flicked open the pages. "It is my diary," said Manuel.

" 'Went with my lord this day to Box Hill,' " read Lord Guy.

"It's not the same book," whispered Peter to Amy.

"That seems to be all right," said Lord Guy, handing it back. "I shall deal with you later, Manuel. Now, my children, your names."

"Peter Jones," said Peter, "and this is my sister, Amy. Don't cry, Amy. It is all right now, you know."

"And where do you live?"

"In Berkeley Square."

"And where is your nursemaid?"

Peter shuffled his feet. "She don't know we're out," he said.

"Then I shall return you to your parents."

"We haven't got any parents," said Peter. "Our big sister looks after us and she's going to be mad." All thoughts of pointing out that Manuel had produced a different book fled from Peter's mind now that he was firmly back in a real world of disapproving grown-ups.

"Better to put up with a little anger from your sister

than to go out wandering again on your own," said Lord Guy. "Manuel, return to Clarges Street and await me. First go over there and tell Mr. Roger I am taking these children home. Come along, children."

The glory of a drive home in a spanking racing curricle was enough to take Peter's mind off his worries.

As he reined in outside the house in Berkeley Square, Lord Guy looked up at it curiously. He felt he had noticed it before, that something monumental had happened to him there.

Then the door opened and Esther hurtled out, eyes only for her brother and sister. When the twins were reported missing, she had risen from her sickbed. She was wearing a loose gown and her red hair was pinned loosely on top of her head.

Lord Guy looked at her in a dazed way.

"You," he said. "You were not a dream. You exist."

"I am grateful to you for bringing the children home," said Esther, not really hearing what he said but looking at him for the first time. Her face stiffened.

"Oh, yes," she said coldly. "We have met."

"Where?" asked Lord Guy.

"You were very drunk. You entered my house one morning and tried to assault me. You have turned Number Sixty-seven Clarges Street into a brothel. I should not even be speaking to you, but I must ask you where you found the children."

"In Hyde Park, ma'am," he said. "They mistook my servant for a spy. He frightened them."

Esther lifted the children down from the carriage, passed them over to the nursery maid, and then turned her attention back to Lord Guy.

"Thank you for returning the children," she said.

She turned away.

"May I see you again?" he said.

She turned back and looked at him blankly.

"Don't be silly," said Miss Esther Jones. And, picking up her skirts, she followed the children into the house and slammed the door.

Chapter Four

"*O Radcliffe! thou once were the charmer*
Of girls who sat reading all night;
Thy heroes were striplings in armour,
Thy heroines damsels in white.

Haut Ton finds her privacy broken,
We trace all her ins and her outs;
The very small talk that is spoken
By very great people at routs.
At Tenby Miss Jinks asks the loan of
The book from the innkeeper's wife,
And reads till she dreams she is one of
The leaders of elegant life.

—THOMAS HAYNES BAYLY

"So that's that," said Lord Guy, pacing up and down. "I've fallen in love with a stern goddess who was witness to the party here, who claims I entered her house when drunk and tried to assault her, and wishes to have nothing to do with me."

Mr. Roger heaved a sentimental sigh. Like quite a number of army officers, he was an incurable romantic.

"It must be a hopeless passion, Guy," he said. "When you go back to the wars, her face will be before your eyes on the battlefield."

"Demne, I want her face before my eyes in bed!"

"No, no, no," said Mr. Roger lugubriously. "Not the thing at all, my dear fellow. You get the strumpets in bed, and if the virtuous and fair won't look at you, you worship them from afar."

"Have you been at the port again?" said Lord Guy testily. "I intend to do something about it. We must turn respectable."

"I don't mind," said Mr. Roger amiably. "Tired already o' card sharps, Pinks of the Ton, and greedy demi-reps."

"We must give another party . . . a rout," said Lord Guy. "It must be all that is elegant."

"If you wish. But this Miss Jones is unlikely to come even if you send the Prince of Wales to fetch her."

"Then I shall find out where she goes, and then try to get myself invitations to the same functions."

"Shouldn't be too difficult," said Mr. Roger. "We're both rich."

"I don't think money will do much to wipe out our black reputation caused by that party."

"Money *and* a title wipe out any stain," said Mr. Roger. "Together they form society's favourite stain remover. How are you going to find out where she goes? Bribe her servants?"

"I shouldn't like to risk that. They might prove honest, and tell her."

"Send Manuel around to ferret out what he can."

Lord Guy frowned. "I am not pleased with Manuel. I do not know what has got into the man since we arrived in England. He pulled a knife on the servants downstairs, and today he terrorised Miss Jones' little brother and sister."

"That's the Spanish for you."

"No, that is *not* the Spanish for you. You must have noticed they are not nearly so cruel to children as the English."

"Where did Manuel come from?"

"He said he was employed in a Portuguese household and that his life was made a misery by the other servants because he was Spanish. We were moving on the next day. He begged me to take him with me as my servant. I agreed. He proved to be quiet and efficient."

"Don't like him. Never have," said Mr. Roger.

"Really, Tommy, one does not like or dislike servants. They are good at their jobs, in which case you keep them on, or bad at their jobs, in which case you get rid of them."

"Don't see it that way," said Mr. Roger. "Nasty servants, however good they are, are unpleasant to have around."

"Well, I can hardly bring the poor fellow all the way to a foreign country and then shove him out to make shift for himself."

"Myself, I would pay his passage back to Spain," said Mr. Roger. "But if you won't use him, how about asking that odd butler of ours, Rainbird. I rather like the fellow. Clever. Got a knowing eye."

"And a disapproving tongue. Very well, make yourself scarce. I can talk to the fellow easier on my own."

Joseph was comfortably seated in The Running Footman, the upper servants' pub, talking to his friend, Luke. Luke worked next door to Number 67 as first footman to Lord Charteris. Luke was tall and handsome and dark-haired in contrast to the tall, blond-haired Joseph. Because of the flour tax, neither footman had powdered his hair.

Joseph had enjoyed his outing in Kensington Gardens with Lizzie. She had a very flattering wide-eyed way of gravely listening to everything he said, which made him feel important. Also, in her clean white dress and with her well-brushed head of shining brown hair, she had looked almost pretty. He wanted to buy her something. He had not yet had time to buy her that present.

"I say, Luke," he said, "what's a genteel thing a fellow can give a lady as a present?"

"Who's it for?" asked Luke curiously.

Joseph coloured and looked away. Like most London servants, he was intensely snobbish. He envied and admired Luke and could not bring himself to say the present was for a mere scullery maid.

"It's for Miss Hunt," he said desperately. Miss Hunt was a rather severe governess who worked at Number 52 Clarges Street.

Luke whistled soundlessly. "Flying high, ain't you?" he said; for a footman to pay court to a governess was as ambitious as a City merchant paying court to a wealthy lady of the ton.

"Never get anywhere if you don't try," said Joseph with a laugh that sounded hollow in his own ears.

"I know just the thing if you've got the ready," said Luke. "A silk rose. Best place to go is Layton & Shear in Covent Garden."

"I don't know as I have time," said Joseph.

"You've bin braggin' as how you got two pounds. Come along. We'll take a hack."

On their return to Clarges Street, the two men carefully stopped the hack at the Piccadilly end so that neither of their butlers should notice their extravagance.

They were strolling along Clarges Street when Luke

suddenly stopped and seized Joseph's arm. "There she is!" he cried. "Miss Hunt. T'other side o' the street."

"I'll wait till tomorrow," said Joseph frantically because he had just spotted Lizzie at the top of the area steps.

"Faint heart never won fair lady," said Luke with a grin. "I'll help you. Miss Hunt!" he called.

A rather hard-featured young woman turned and stared haughtily.

Joseph groaned inwardly. He had to go through with it. There was no way he could bring himself to tell Luke he had bought an expensive silk rose for a mere scullery maid.

He crossed the road with Luke at his heels. "Miss Hunt," said Joseph with a deep bow, "pray do me the honour of eccepting this here rose." She raised thin brows and looked at him as if he had crept out of a sewer. "It's silk," gabbled Joseph.

She stared coldly at Joseph, raking him from head to foot, before turning away and mounting the steps.

"Garn, you old ratbag," called Luke in a fury. "I bets you wear dirty drawers."

"I shall speak to your employers," said Miss Hunt. "Disgusting jackanapes!"

"That's torn it," said Joseph savagely. "Wot you say that for, yer bleeding kennel mouff?"

"She asked for it," said Luke passionately. "See if I care. If you ask me, you'd be a curst sight better off with that Lizzie over there. Turning into a right looker, she is."

Luke saw his butler, Mr. Blenkinsop, peering out of a downstairs window of Number 65, and leapt across the road and vanished inside.

Joseph walked miserably over to where Lizzie was standing, watching him sorrowfully.

"What are you staring at me for?" he demanded angrily. He shouldered his way rudely past her and went down the stairs.

Rainbird listened with outward courtesy and inward growing amusement to Lord Guy's question as to whether the butler knew anything about a Miss Jones of Berkeley Square.

"As a matter of fact, I do," said Rainbird. "I had the honour to be entertained to tea by Miss Jones."

"And how did that come about?" asked Lord Guy.

Rainbird explained about Miss Jones' meeting with Lizzie and about the lady's desire to impart education to her servants. "It appears," added Rainbird, "that Miss Jones does not go anywhere socially. I thought it a pity that such a fine-looking lady should lead such an isolated life. I suggested Miss Jones might consider the future of the children. Should she wish good marriages for them, it might be in their interest if Miss Jones were to gain an entrée to the ton."

"And what did she say to that?"

"Miss Jones said the children were still young, but she appeared to be considering the matter. Moreover, she appeared intrigued with my suggestion that there was no reason why education should be not be fun. Perhaps Miss Jones may venture to take the children to some London amusement."

"Miss Jones has taken me in dislike, Rainbird."

"Indeed, my lord."

"I cannot call on her formally. I would like to meet her by accident. You and your 'family,' as you call them, may take all the free time you want if you can contrive to find out where she plans to go—if there is some public place where I can accidentally come across her."

"Certainly, my lord. Very good, my lord."

"Does not my request strike you as strange?"

"It is not my place to say so, my lord."

"You have my permission to forget your place."

"In that case, my lord, I would like to take leave to tell you, I consider you are behaving in a most sensible manner. Miss Jones is a trifle strict, but she is a good lady."

"Which makes my task all the more difficult."

"I think, my lord, Miss Jones would not find it at all odd were I to call again to present her with a few suitable books."

"Go to it," said Lord Guy, "and report to me as soon as you have any news."

The servants were intrigued and delighted at this odd turn of events. Miss Jones had been heaven-sent, they said.

"But," cautioned Jenny, resting her sharp chin on her red hands, "you'd better start off and do your best, Mr. Rainbird, 'fore he gets disappointed and starts kicking up his heels again."

Rainbird was received in Berkeley Square the following day by a Miss Jones who was rather red about the nose and eyes, since she was still suffering from the cold.

She accepted the books Rainbird had brought with delight. "Your idea is already most successful," she said warmly. "The female servants are begging for more romances. I read one myself," said Miss Jones, "and was amazed to find it most entertaining. I also feel I have been over-strict with the children. Too many lessons can be as bad as too few. I am taking them to Astley's Amphitheatre tomorrow evening."

Astley's was a popular combination of circus and drama and spectacle on the Surrey side of the river.

Light-hearted with such early success, Rainbird returned to Lord Guy with the news. Lord Guy sent him out again to purchase two of the best seats at Astley's. It never dawned on him that Miss Jones might sit anywhere else.

But Esther had given in to Peter's pleadings to get "as near as possible" and had booked three places in one of the front benches.

When Esther arrived at Astley's and was alarmed to find herself the only woman on the front benches and surrounded by noisy bucks, she soon quelled any advances with an icy stare. Clutching her umbrella in case she should need to use it as a weapon, she settled down to enjoy the show.

It was a mixture of the vulgar and sentimental. The first piece was about a wicked landlord throwing a pretty maiden and her widowed mother out into the snow. Tinsel snow drifted down on the stage. The heroine looked very fragile and pretty and wept most becomingly. "What a lot of nonsense," Esther told herself, irritated to feel a lump rising in her throat. The hero entered, magnificent in gold braid and top boots. How the children cheered!

Far behind Esther in a side box, Lord Guy put down his opera glasses and said to Mr. Roger, "She's right on the front bench!"

"You *sure* she's a lady?" exclaimed Mr. Roger.

"Yes, most definitely. I only hope the gentlemen about her realise that."

"She's big, I'll grant you that," said Mr. Roger, looking through his opera telescope. "But that hat's enough to frighten anyone."

Esther was wearing an unbecoming black slouch hat that drooped down the back of her neck.

The noisy bucks around her, who had been discussing her loudly while all her interest had been in the drama, had finally put her down as a dragon of a governess, one who would make a deuce of a scene if they became too warm in their attentions.

If Esther had been left in peace to enjoy the show, it is doubtful if she would have had anything at all to do with Lord Guy Carlton in the future. But backstage, the Fates were twisting things to make them happen otherwise.

Madame Chartreuse, that famous equestrienne, was preparing to make her entrance. The piece was quite simple. A gypsy stole her child, who was represented by a large doll. The villain threw the "child" down on a pile of sacks in the glade where he and his brigands hid out from the law. In rode Madame Chartreuse, standing up in the saddle of her white horse. Crouching down, she seized the "child" and rode off. Applause and curtain. Or rather, that was the way it was supposed to be.

But her manager, Silas Manchester, who had been in love with her for years, had discovered she had fallen in love with a young actor in the cast. He taxed her with it before she was about to go on. She laughed in his face and said she was tired of him.

The piece started. The villain snatched the child from her. She wept, her "mother" wept, and the snow fell, because they had tinsel snow left over. Next scene. The doll was placed by the villain on the pile of sacks. Silas Manchester, on his hands and knees, slid a cane onto the stage, hooked the handle round the large doll's neck, and gently drew it offstage. Then he stood back to watch the fury on his love's face when she found her act had been ruined.

Now, the doll was life-sized and had red curls.

One split second after she had ridden onto the stage, wearing a spangled tutu and flesh-coloured tights, Madame Chartreuse's sharp eyes noticed the missing doll. In the next second, she noticed Peter with his red curls sitting on the front bench. That any respectable child would be brought to sit in the front benches, which were usually only occupied by men who came to ogle the female performers, never crossed her mind, or she would not have done what she did next.

She rode round in a circle, standing on the horse. The stage was a sort of half-circus ring on a level with the front benches. Then, with one quick movement, she crouched down, put out one muscular arm, and lifted little Peter up into the saddle to stand next to her.

Dazzled and excited, Peter clutched hold of one of her plump legs and hung on tight with one hand and waved frantically to Esther with the other.

"Odds Fish," said Mr. Roger, "that's torn it." Lord Guy had already vaulted over the box and was making his way rapidly to the front.

Madame Chartreuse jumped down lightly, holding Peter, placed him beside her, and took a bow to tumultuous applause while her manager gnashed his teeth in the wings and looked more like a stage villain than any of the actors.

Miss Esther Jones' temper, so long held firmly in check, flamed up. Seizing her umbrella, she marched on the stage and brought it down full on Madame Chartreuse's head, took Peter by the hand, and began to march back to her seat. Madame Chartreuse jumped on Esther's back, tore her hat off, and threw it in the sawdust, leapt down and began to do a sort of war dance on it. Esther, the glory of her red hair now spilling about her shoulders, placed Peter beside his sister, told him sternly not to move, marched back to Madame and slapped her with such force that the actress went flying. Madame Chartreuse rose to her feet, her eyes blazing with hate.

"A mill! A mill!" cheered the audience wildly. "A hundred to one on the Amazon!" cried one buck, delirious with joy as he stared as Esther. "Look at those shoulders!" he called.

Lord Guy ran onto the stage just as the two women

were about to close again. He seized both their hands in a powerful grip and dragged them round to face the audience.

"Bow!" he said savagely. "Bow, damn the pair of you."

In a dazed way, Esther bowed. Madame Chartreuse, quickly grasping the advantages of the situation, bowed as well.

What a roar of applause went up! Money and jewels were thrown in the ring.

Everyone in the audience thought the whole scene had been deliberately staged.

Esther began to shiver and feel sick. What had she done? Amy and Peter were dancing up and down on the front benches, cheering themselves hoarse.

"Get the children," said Lord Guy in Esther's ear. "It is time to go."

With a graceful wave to the crowd, he released Madame Chartreuse's hand, but kept a firm grip on Esther's. Weakly, she let herself be led up the centre aisle while Peter and Amy held on to Lord Guy's coat-tails. It was like walking through a tunnel of sound, a thin lane through a forest of clapping hands.

At one point, Mr. Roger thrust his way forward and looked about to join them, but Lord Guy shook his head.

Outside in the street, Esther stood trembling with her head bowed. "Where is your carriage?" demanded Lord Guy.

"I came in a hack."

"Manuel," called Lord Guy. His servant appeared at his elbow. "My carriage, immediately," said Lord Guy.

Peter and Amy had fallen silent. They looked anxiously up at their big sister. Something had gone badly wrong. But they still thought that in some clever and amazing way Esther had planned the whole thing.

"Please leave me, my lord," said Esther quietly.

"Think of the children," he said. "The evening air is cold. I have a closed carriage."

She said nothing more but continued to stand with her head bowed, her heavy red hair concealing her face.

Lord Guy was grateful he had hired a closed carriage for the Season. His racing curricle was all very well for fine weather, but unsuitable for an evening outing in this wintry spring.

He handed her in, then the children, and told the coachman to drive them to Berkeley Square.

Esther felt ready to sink with shame. She had behaved like a washerwoman in front of a good section of London, and now she was allowing herself and the dear children to be escorted home by a rake and libertine.

"Did you enjoy your evening, children?" she heard Lord Guy ask.

"It was the most wonderful evening of my life," said Peter solemnly. "How clever of you, Esther, to arrange *such* a treat."

Esther raised her eyes and opened her mouth to explain, but by the light of the carriage candle lamp in its clockwork holder, she saw Lord Guy gently shake his head.

"As long as you enjoyed it," she said stiffly.

Amy hugged her big sister. "I *love* you, Esther," she said. "I've never been so happy."

Esther turned her head away and blinked back a sudden rush of tears. She led a lonely life and did as much for the children as she possibly could. She had always wanted them to show some demonstration of love. One monumental piece of disgraceful behavior had elicited all the protestations of affection of which she had dreamt.

"Me, too," said Peter, pressing her hand. "I was so proud of you, Esther, I thought my heart would burst. And you *trusted* me. I felt like a man when she picked me up on that horse. And that stage fight you had with her was so *real.* It was monstrous clever the way she fell back when you pretended to strike her."

When the carriage reached Berkeley Square, Esther squared her shoulders, and, avoiding Lord Guy's eye, said stiffly, "I am much indebted to you, sir."

"Delighted to be of service, ma'am," he said.

Esther wanted rid of him, but at the same time she craved reassurance from some member of society, be it only a soiled and degraded one.

"May I offer you some refreshment, my lord?" she said.

"Thank you. You are very kind."

Once indoors, Esther put him in the dim and dark saloon and took the excited children upstairs. Before she turned them over to the nursery maid, she begged them not to tell any of the servants, "for it was a most wild and unconventional thing to do," she ended uncomfortably.

"We won't tell a soul, will we, Amy?" said Peter. "You've never given us a big secret to keep before, Esther."

Once she had called the nursery maid, Esther rang for her own maid and, with her help, changed her gown and put her hair into a knot, shoved one of her caps firmly on top, and went down the stairs again to face Lord Guy.

It was an evening for breaking the conventions. Esther knew, as she was unmarried and unchaperoned, she should have left the door open. But she was frightened of one of the servants hearing what she had to say, and so, once she had ascertained that wine and cakes had been brought in, she closed the door.

Lord Guy poured her a glass of wine and handed it to her. Esther was about to point out that she had never in her life had anything stronger than lemonade, but she was still shaken, and so she took the glass and asked Lord Guy to sit down.

"I gather you do not use this room much, ma'am," said Lord Guy, sitting down on an uncomfortable high-backed and carved Jacobean monstrosity.

"On the contrary," said Esther, automatically sipping her wine, "it is in constant use."

Lord Guy looked about. The room was dominated by a sort of pulpit with a large Bible on it. The curtains at the windows were as heavy and red and stiff as if they had been steeped in blood. The mantelpiece was of black marble, as was the clock on it. There was a painting above the fireplace of a cross-looking man in severe clothes who was pointing solemnly at his ear, rather as if to show a doctor where it hurt, or to indicate the whole world was mad.

"Your father?" asked Lord Guy politely.

"No, my lord," said Esther with a return to her usual manner. "That is one of our great evangelical reformers, Mr. Isaac Sidcup."

He noticed she had drunk almost all of her wine, and refilled her glass.

He sat down again and crossed a pair of well-moulded legs. *People went on about present-day women's fashions being indecent,* thought Esther. *But the men wear their Inexpressibles so skin-tight, they leave little to the imagination.*

She frowned suspiciously at her wineglass. Was this why the preachers warned against the pernicious effects of wine? Was it the wine that was causing her to think about men's legs?

Esther looked up and saw Lord Guy was studying her with a mixture of tenderness and amusement. *He is very handsome,* she thought breathlessly.

With an obvious effort, she pulled herself together.

"My lord," she said, "I trust you will not speak of the

happenings tonight or that I entertained you without a chaperone."

"You have my solemn word."

"On the other hand, I do not see how it can be kept quiet. The whole of London will be talking about it tomorrow."

"They will gossip furiously about what appeared to be an exciting theatrical performance. They will not believe the actress they saw is a respectable lady, living in Berkeley Square. Avoid social engagements for a week. After that, everyone will have forgotten about it."

"I have no social engagements," said Esther. "Your unusual and estimable butler suggested perhaps I should look to the future—the children's future—and make some friends in the ton. I am not of the aristocracy."

"You are obviously of the gentry. You will not find any doors closed to you—if you go about it the right way."

"And what is the right way?"

"I suggest you hold an entertainment and ask my butler how to go about it. It appears one must have a theme, decorate the rooms, and provide an entertainment which will intrigue society."

"But I do not know anyone!"

"Send out richly embossed invitations. London is thin of amusements. Rainbird will know whom you should invite."

"You are most kind." Esther rose to her feet as a signal that the call was at an end.

"May I call on you, ma'am?" asked Lord Guy.

"I cannot allow that," said Esther gravely. "I have the children's morals to consider. I fear you are a rake."

"Rakes can reform."

Esther shook her head, unconsciously echoing Rainbird. "That only happens in books, my lord," she said sadly. "Only in books."

Lord Guy dismissed the carriage and walked slowly back to Clarges Street. Damn that supper party! Was he never to be free of the scandal that had caused?

Rainbird was waiting for him in the hall.

"Good evening, my lord," he said, taking Lord Guy's cloak and seemingly oblivious to Manuel, who stood scowling in the shadows.

"Good evening, Rainbird. Mr. Roger at home?"

"He is not yet returned."

"Good. Come with me, Rainbird. You must return to Berkeley Square as soon as possible."

Chapter
Five

'Come, come,' said Tom's father, 'at your time of
* life,*
'There's no longer excuse for thus playing the rake—
'It is time you should think, boy, of taking a wife'—
'Why, so it is, father—whose wife shall I take?'

—THOMAS MOORE

Once more Rainbird sat facing Miss Esther Jones. He politely asked if she had enjoyed Astley's and was surprised to see that his innocent question had brought a blush to her cheeks.

He quickly changed the subject and asked how he could be of service to her.

"I do not know what your master has told you," said Esther, "but the fact is I am desirous of taking your advice and introducing myself to the ton."

"I have given the matter careful thought," said Rainbird, "for my lord did mention the matter to me. I think a children's party would be a good idea. There are many tonnish children in Berkeley Square."

"What a wonderful idea!" cried Esther. Then her face fell. "But how do I go about inviting them? I regret to say I have not allowed Peter or Amy to play with any children."

"It will be necessary for me to prepare the ground first," said Rainbird. "To that end, I must ask you two seemingly impertinent questions."

"Go ahead."

"Are you engaged to be married?"

"No, Mr. Rainbird."

Rainbird smiled with pleasure at the flattering use of that little word "Mr." in front of his name. The small courtesy meant more to him than any lavish tip.

"And," he pursued, "are you in comfortable circumstances?"

"Very. I regret to confess to one sin. I gamble on 'Change. It is said in the City that my wealth rivals that of Rothschild."

"May I say, then, Miss Jones, you will have no trouble at all in attracting the attention of the ton when such facts are made known."

"Are they *all* so mercenary?"

"In the main, yes. Of course, my master has a mind above such worldly things," said Rainbird, tilting his head on one side and looking at her searchingly.

But Esther did not rise to the bait. "And how do you go about broadcasting such tempting facts? You can hardly take an advertisement in the *Morning Post*."

"Servants' gossip is very useful if cleverly used," said Rainbird. "Tonight I will go out drinking and gossiping. By tomorrow, the whole of Berkeley Square will know of the existence of Miss Jones."

"And then I shall send out my invitations to a children's party," cried Esther, her eyes shining. "It is a wonderful idea!"

"What a deuced stupid idea," said Lord Guy crossly after Rainbird had reported back to him. "A children's party! Of what use is that to me?"

"Have you ever attended a ton children's party, my lord?" asked Rainbird.

"No. Have you?"

"Yes, my lord. Before I went into service, I worked as an acrobat on the fairgrounds, also as a magician and juggler. I came to London and hired myself out as an entertainer for children's parties. It nigh broke my spirit."

A wicked gleam entered Lord Guy's eye. "And does the fair Miss Jones know what she is in for?"

"No, my lord. She has only seen the children of Mayfair accompanied by strict nannies and governesses. She has never seen what the little darlings are like when they are with their fond mamas."

"And where do I come in?"

"I think, my lord, you come in just about half an hour after the party has begun. I shall be looking for you as you fortuitously happen to be strolling past."

"And I leap to the rescue?"

"Yes, my lord. You step in with a firm hand and a stern moralising tone."

"Have *you* been invited?" asked Lord Guy. This butler was an attractive fellow with his trim figure and humourous face. Could Miss Jones . . . ? Lord Guy almost swore. He was becoming jealous of a servant.

"Yes, my lord," said Rainbird. "I am the entertainer. Angus MacGregor, your lordship's chef, has been engaged for the day. He is wonderful at making elaborate confectionery."

"Has Miss Jones not managed to train her servants properly that she needs must borrow mine?"

"It takes a certain type of servant," said Rainbird. "We are not all alike, my lord."

"No, I can see that. It was uncharitable of me."

"Joseph is to serve the ices and jellies to the children."

Rainbird studied the ceiling. "Joseph is a sensitive creature and brings out the worst in women and children."

The street door knocker began to sound.

"Let Manuel answer that," said Lord Guy.

"Your servant went out, my lord, just after you arrived home."

"Then send whoever it is away. I am in no mood for callers."

Rainbird came back a few minutes later with a silver card on a tray, which he presented to Lord Guy.

"It is a Lady Debenham," he said, "with her children's governess. She insists on seeing your lordship. She claims her governess was grossly insulted by Joseph."

"That is Joseph of the sensitive nature?"

"Yes, my lord."

"Must I see her?"

"That is for you to say, my lord," said Rainbird. "Lady Debenham lives at Number Fifty-two."

"Very well. Bring her in. And Joseph."

Lord Guy rose to his feet as Lady Debenham entered the room.

She looked remarkably like her governess, being harsh of feature and haughty of manner. She sat down primly, and Miss Hunt stood to attention behind her chair.

"I would not have come here had I not felt strongly over the insult to my poor Miss Hunt," began Lady Debenham.

Joseph sidled in and stood looking wretched.

"Pray tell me what happened, Lady Debenham," said Lord Guy.

"Your footman, accompanied by another footman, approached Miss Hunt. Your footman had the impertinence to present her with a silk rose, which she, of course, refused. One of them shouted something frightful at her.

Miss Hunt has great sensibility. She had a Spasm as soon as she was safely inside the house.

"It offends *my* sensibilities to have to set foot inside *this* house, my lord. I take leave to tell you, you have brought shame on Mayfair with your antics. I take further leave to tell you—"

Lord Guy raised a hand.

"Enough!" he said. "Joseph, come here! What exactly was said by you or this other footman?"

"It wasn't me, honest, my lord. It was Luke," said Joseph, shuffling forward and standing with his head bowed.

"Raise your head, man, when you address me!"

Joseph raised his head. There was the glint of tears in his eyes and his lip was trembling.

"I ask you again, what did this fellow, Luke, say?"

"I give . . . gave a silk rose to Miss Hunt, as a present, like," said Joseph miserably. "She said nothink, just raised her eyebrows and turned her back. Luke, he . . . he . . ."

"Come on. Come on. Out with it!"

"He said, 'I bets you w-wears d-dirty d-drawers,'" said Joseph, beginning to sob.

Lord Guy took out his quizzing glass, polished it, raised it to one eye and thoughtfully studied the iron-faced Miss Hunt.

"And do you?" he asked mildly.

"My lord?" said Miss Hunt.

"Do you wear dirty drawers?"

Rainbird turned quickly away to hide a smile. Joseph's mouth dropped open.

Lady Debenham began to make strange puffing noises, like one of the new steam engines. Then, out of all the chugging and puffing, her voice suddenly screamed, "How *dare* you?"

"If you walk into my house and insult me," said Lord Guy indifferently, "then you must expect to be insulted in return."

"You, my lord, are as bad as your servants."

"And you, my lady, are a sour-faced, ungracious, Friday-faced frump, just like *your* servant."

"Come, Miss Hunt," cried Lady Debenham.

"I feel a Spasm coming on," faltered Miss Hunt.

"Pull yourself together," snapped Lady Debenham. "It is I who is entitled to have a Spasm, not you."

She swept out, nearly colliding with Rainbird as he leapt to hold the door open for her.

Rainbird saw them out and returned to the front parlour. *I must not laugh,* he thought, but laughter was bubbling up inside him.

"Now, Joseph," said Lord Guy, "it seems you were wrong in your choice of friend and in your choice of inamorata. What on earth made you want to give an expensive present to a nasty woman like that?"

Joseph hung his head. "It wasn't really for her, my lord. It was for Lizzie."

Lizzie? thought Lord Guy. Then his face cleared. Lizzie was the scullery maid who had so impressed Miss Jones.

"Ah," he said, "our Lizzie is by way of being something of a catalyst."

"No, my lord," said Joseph. "Lizzie's a Roman Catholic."

"Well, if you bought the rose for Lizzie, why give it to Miss Hunt?"

"I lied to Luke, my lord. Luke is Lord Charteris', next doors', first footman. I couldn't tell him it was for Lizzie, me being a footman, my lord."

"Why not?"

Joseph blushed and remained silent. Rainbird stepped

into the breach. "What Joseph is trying to say, my lord, is that a scullery maid in the hierarchy of the servants' hall is far beneath a footman. It would be rather like your lordship buying a genteel present for a tavern wench."

Lord Guy blinked. He had often found himself becoming impatient with the snobberies of the ton. He had never guessed that such rigid divisions of caste existed belowstairs.

"I cannot chastise Luke," said Lord Guy. "That is a job for Lord Charteris. You are infuriating, you know. I don't know what came over me. I have never been so rude to a lady in the whole of my life. Get out of here and consider yourself lucky that I don't complain to the Duke of Pelham's agent about you."

"Thank you, my lord," said Joseph, scuttling off.

Lord Guy turned to the butler. "Now, Rainbird," he began. He broke off. Rainbird's face was twitching, and his eyes glistened with tears.

"Oh, laugh, if you want to," sighed Lord Guy.

Rainbird began to laugh. It started off as a restrained titter and ended up as a guffaw. He laughed helplessly, holding his sides, the tears streaming down his cheeks.

Lord Guy began to laugh as well. He was laughing because Rainbird's laughter was infectious, and the world was suddenly a glittering and wonderful place because of the very existence of one stern goddess of Berkeley Square.

The servants had a brief account of what had happened from Joseph—although Joseph did not say the present had really been for Lizzie. The presence of Manuel, who slid round the door and joined them, put a damper on the conversation. They were wondering how to get rid of him when Rainbird joined them and said to Manuel, "Have you been mucking about with the newspaper?"

"Please. I do not understand," said Manuel.

"It's like this. The *Morning Post* and the *News* are delivered daily. When his lordship has finished with them, he gives them to me to take down to the servants. Angus said that an article had been cut out of one of the papers with scissors."

Manuel shrugged. "His lordship, he want it for something."

"It was not his lordship. I asked him. It wasn't one of us, so that leaves you."

"I go," said Manuel, and vanished out the door.

"Odd," said Rainbird. "But that's got rid of him. Wait till you hear this!"

The servants roared with laughter over the insult to Lady Debenham and her governess—with the exception of Lizzie, who was still hurt. Rainbird thought Joseph should tell Lizzie himself that he had really bought the rose for her and so left out that part of it.

Then he told them about his interview with Miss Jones.

They laughed and gossiped and plotted. Joseph got out his mandolin and began to strum a lively song.

Lord Guy and Mr. Roger, stepping out, paused to listen to the sounds of merriment drifting up from the basement.

"I tell you, Tommy," said Lord Guy, "there's a whole other life goes on down there."

Esther had told her business managers, the gentlemen who "fronted" for her in the buying and selling of stocks and shares, that she would do no further work until the Season was over.

Up until recently, money had been security. The very sight of her father throwing it away on frivolous trifles had eaten into her soul. But now, for Peter's and Amy's sake, she reminded herself sternly, it was time to unloosen the purse strings.

For the first time in her life, she felt the need of a female companion badly. Her father's scandalous mode of living had set her apart from the young ladies of the neighbourhood when she was growing up. Now she wished she had someone to help her choose clothes.

But she gritted her teeth and summoned London's leading dressmaker to Berkeley Square and ordered a new wardrobe. She applied for, and got, a box at the opera, not knowing that, had it not been for Rainbird's timely gossip, she would have been turned down by the stern committee who kept the Italian Opera as exclusive as Almack's Assembly Rooms.

Although she had reached the great age of twenty-six, put on caps, and resigned herself to a life as a spinster, Esther knew that she would be damned as eccentric if she made her appearance at the opera unescorted. In despair, she sent for Rainbird, the only person she knew who might be able to solve her problem.

As far as the children's party was concerned, at least, all seemed set for success. The invitations had gone out, and had all been accepted.

While Esther worried about making her social début, Lord Guy had received a sharp setback to his own plans.

A middle-aged cousin he only vaguely remembered arrived on his doorstep, complete with luggage, carrying a letter from his father, the Earl of Cramworth. Her name was Miss Ruth Fipps. She was fat, pleasant and faded, and sure of her welcome.

"Your father will explain everything," she said. "That nice housekeeper, Mrs. Middleton, suggests I should take the large bedroom next to the dining room while you and Mr. Roger share the bedrooms on the next floor."

"She did, did she?" said Lord Guy pleasantly, although he was wishing Miss Fipps would disappear. He waited until Alice had served his cousin with tea and left the room, and then he opened the letter from his father.

The earl wrote that he had received Guy's letter from Portugal giving his proposed address in London. He went on to give a great deal of rambling gossip about the estate, and ended, "I am sending you Miss Fipps, your cousin, and one of our poor relations. I have had her with me this age, and feel it is time you shared some of the responsibility of looking after the family incumbents. If you are still suffering from the effects of the fever, she can help to nurse you. I may also be sending you your Great Aunt Josephine. If, however, you have decided to please me by taking a wife—and I do not mean someone else's wife—I shall send for Miss Fipps and spare you Great Aunt Josephine's presence."

Lord Guy put down the letter and smiled bleakly at Miss Fipps, who nodded vaguely and smiled back.

Rainbird entered the room. "May I beg a word with you in private, my lord?" he said.

Sure it was more news of his beloved, Lord Guy made his excuses to his cousin and drew Rainbird out into the hall.

"My lord," said Rainbird in a low voice. "Miss Jones has once again asked my advice."

"On what?"

"Miss Jones wishes to launch herself on society and is in need of a genteel female companion." Rainbird looked meaningfully at the closed parlour door. "And you, my lord, have an unexpected visit from a cousin."

"Have you heard of Machiavelli, Rainbird?"

"Yes, my lord. Some Italian, was he not?"

"Yes, he was. Wait here."

Lord Guy pinned a winning smile on his face and went back into the parlour. "My dear Miss Fipps," he said. "My *very* dear Miss Fipps. I wish you to perform a service for me which will enable you to earn a comfortable sum of money. . . ."

Chapter
Six

They laugh, and are glad, and are terrible.

—HEBRIDEAN FOLK SONG

The day of Esther's children's party dawned cold and bright.

Rainbird, Angus, and Joseph were at Berkeley Square early in the morning to begin the preparations. As well as confections for the children, cakes, ratafia, champagne, and negus had to be set out for their mothers.

The party would take place in the downstairs saloon. The mothers were expected to retire and take refreshment in the upstairs drawing room. The party was to begin at two and end at four. Lord Guy was to stroll past the house at two-thirty precisely.

Miss Fipps, hired as companion to Esther, was not in on the plot. She had been told to conceal her relationship to Lord Guy. To enable her to remember this vital fact, Lord Guy had paid her a substantial sum of money. Esther, who normally would not have dreamt of engaging anyone without demanding and checking references thoroughly, was so anxious to begin her début and too grateful to Rainbird for having produced such a suitable lady at such short notice, that she had hired Miss Fipps after questioning her only for some ten minutes.

So Lord Guy's cousin found herself in comfortable circumstances and with money in her reticule for the first time in her life. She was placid and undemanding, but she loved food in great quantities and had found the Earl of Cramworth's table too stingy for her tastes. Being a poor relation, she was used to fitting quietly into different households. She was one of those ladies who have absolutely no taste whatsoever when it comes to dressing herself but have a sharp eye for what will best flatter someone else. Esther was persuaded to cancel several gowns because of what Miss Fipps described as "an unfortunate choice of colour." She was highly flattered when Esther bowed before her superior wisdom and cancelled two pink gowns, one of dark purple, and another one in a depressing shade of mud-brown.

All seemed set fair for Rainbird's campaign.

And then, just after the butler had left that morning, Lord Guy was summoned to Horse Guards.

"What do they want?" asked Mr. Roger.

"Might be out to try to get Wellington. These military men in Horse Guards always think they can run battles from London better than the commander on the spot," said Lord Guy. "Or, of course, it could be that scandal of his brother's."

Wellington's brother, Richard, Lord Wellesley, had caused a royal fuss when he had taken out to Spain, in great pomp and circumstance, in a separate ship hired for the purpose, a common whore called Sally Douglas.

"I only hope I am not kept kicking my heels," said Lord Guy. "It is General Warren Thomson who has sent for me. He is an old man, and the old men still think Wellington a young hothead."

When the two friends reached the military headquarters at Horse Guards, Lord Guy was told he must wait. After pacing up and down an ante-room for an hour, Lord Guy was eventually summoned through to the general's office. Mr. Roger settled himself down to wait. His eyes were beginning to droop and his head to nod when he thought he saw Manuel standing with his ear pressed to the door.

He jerked bolt upright and opened his eyes wide. But Manuel was standing over by the window, moodily staring out.

Mr. Roger looked at the Spanish servant. Surely he could not have moved *that* quickly. He, Tommy Roger, must have been imagining things. But just to be sure . . .

"Hey, Manuel," he said. "Run out and buy me some cheroots. Looks as if it's going to be a long wait."

Manuel stood quite still, his eyes blank. For one minute Mr. Roger thought he was going to refuse to go. Then, with a little shrug, he bowed and left.

Mr. Roger picked up his chair, carried it over to the general's door, leaned it against it, and settled himself comfortably. He really must have a word with Guy about that Spaniard was his last thought before he fell asleep.

On Rainbird's instructions, Esther had invited five ladies and their children. The children, ranging in age from three to fourteen, numbered twenty. Lady Partlett had five, Mrs. Havers-Dunese, six; the Countess of Resway, two; Mrs. Dunstable, four; and the Honourable Clara ffrench, three.

All five ladies were extremely modishly dressed, although brittle-voiced and evasive of eye. Their glances slid this way and that as they assessed the value of the furniture, the curtains, and Esther's new gown—a becoming green crêpe. Esther's hair had been dressed à la Grecque. With her great height and her beautiful, if somewhat stern, features, she looked more like the goddess of Lord Guy's dreams than ever.

The children were herded into the downstairs saloon and told to behave themselves and enjoy the entertainment. Esther, who wanted to stay to watch Rainbird's performance, found to her disappointment she was expected to entertain the mothers in the drawing-room.

The five ladies exclaimed with many flattering coos of delight over the splendour of the delicacies prepared for them and the excellence of the champagne. Then they turned their attention to their hostess. They clustered around her like so many elegant and exotic birds of prey, particularly as feathers were in fashion that Season. The Countess of Resway, her scrawny neck rising like that of a vulture from a collar of white marabou, was the first to realise that Esther was socially ignorant of who was what and what was what in tonnish circles.

"My dear Miss Jones," she said, demolishing seed cake with little pecking movements of her lips, "you *must* know dear George."

"Dear George" was Mr. Brummell, that famous arbiter of fashion, but Esther, unused to this tactic of dropping the first names of famous people, looked blank.

"I am afraid I know hardly anyone," said Esther meekly.

Their eyes shone with delight. With many "oh-my-dear-but-you-musts" they set about the delicious task of making Esther feel like a provincial dowd. So great was her mortification that it was some time before she began to hear the tremendous screams and yells and bumps coming from downstairs.

She was about to rise and go to see what was happening, when vague Miss Fipps cleared her throat and unexpectedly rose to Esther's defence. Esther could not believe it. She had regarded Miss Fipps as a necessary appendage but had never thought of her in the role of champion.

She would have been startled and touched could she have known that Miss Fipps never before had entered the lists, but that the middle-aged spinster had rapidly become very fond of her indeed.

"Miss Jones does not know anyone as yet," said Miss Fipps. "The reason for this is because Miss Jones is the richest woman in England and has to fight shy of toad-eaters, counter-jumpers, and impoverished members of the ton. She sets very high standards of behaviour for herself and others. She does not *need* the approval of society. But society is on trial today in her eyes, ladies. It is up to you whether she forms a good opinion of the ton or not."

Esther forced herself to look calm and stately. The ladies at first bridled at the idea of anyone putting *them* on trial. But the magic words that they had half put down to exaggerated servants' gossip rang in their ears like a siren's song—"the richest woman in England."

They all did a quick about-turn and began to promise invitations, to praise Esther's gown, her manner, her hair, and her home until she felt every bit as uncomfortable as she had done when they were being thoroughly nasty.

Then the door of the drawing-room swung open, and Peter stood there, bespattered with cake.

"Come quickly, Esther," he cried. "They are breaking up our home. They are savages!"

"Hair!" said Lord Guy savagely as he and Mr. Roger drove furiously in the direction of Berkeley Square. "Hair! That's all the old fool wanted to talk about. He went on for *hours*. Why had Wellington got rid of the famous British army pigtail? It was demoralising the forces. It was giving power to Napoleon. I said it was simply a matter of hygiene. Each man now has to have his head cropped close, and it has to be sponged every day. He said all this washing was insane. What was all this fuss about a few little grey gentlemen—by which he meant lice. Had them himself, said the dirty old . . . general, producing a scratcher and stirring them about on his head right in front of me."

"Well, at least Manuel couldn't have heard any military secrets," said Mr. Roger.

"What do you mean?"

"Swear I nearly caught the chap with his ear at the door, but I might be mistaken. Anyway, I sent him out for cheroots and blocked the door myself."

"Don't start suspecting Manuel of being a spy. According to everyone in London, every foreigner is a spy. They set on some poor old French emigré yesterday at King's Cross and half killed him."

"All the same," began Mr. Roger with a worried frown.

"Never mind," interrupted Lord Guy. "Here we are, and fifteen minutes late."

From the house in Berkeley Square came the sounds of screaming women and breaking glass.

Once more, Lord Guy opened the door and strode in uninvited. He walked straight into the battlefield in the saloon.

Children were shouting and crying and throwing jellies. Esther was holding a kicking, screaming child of six under one arm while the child's diminutive mother—Mrs. Havers-Dunese—jumped up and down, calling her a murderess, trying to snatch her child back with one hand and scratch Esther's face with the other.

The Countess of Resway was in a faint, and her lady's maid was trying to holding burning feathers under her nose while an angel-faced moppet stuffed a cream cake into the brim of the distracted maid's hat.

The table-cloth on the long table at one end of the room which had held the food had been half dragged off. Three tots were sitting amongst the wreckage, howling like banshees, while the older children whooped about the room like Red Indians on the warpath.

Esther saw Lord Guy Carlton. It was too much, she thought. She was about to scream to him to get out when she realised an uncanny silence had fallen on the room. Yet he did nothing. He simply stood there, in all the elegance of Weston's tailoring, in all the starched whiteness of fine linen, in all the glory of embroidered waistcoat, leather breeches, and top-boots like black glass, and surveyed the appalling scene through his quizzing glass.

The children were staring at him in open-mouthed silence. The Countess of Resway had snapped out of her faint, thrust her maid and feathers away, and had started to pat her hair. Mrs. Havers-Dunese was smiling coyly; Mrs. Dunstable was striking her best Attitude, that of Artemis, hand shading the brow and one foot lifted out behind her; the Honourable Clara ffrench had turned away and was surreptitiously poking loose tendrils of hair back up under her hat; and Lady Partlett was pouting archly and waving her hands in a deprecating way as if to indicate it all had nothing to do with her.

Lord Guy let his quizzing glass fall. He looked at the eldest child, Bartholomew Dunstable, a gawky fourteen-year-old, and crooked his finger.

Bartholomew meekly came to stand in front of him.

"I elect you the captain of this regiment," said Lord Guy. "Miss Jones will summon her housemaids, who will give each child dustpans, brushes, cloths, and bowls of water. When this room is completely cleaned, you will inform Miss Jones of the fact. Do you understand?"

"Yes, sir," said Bartholomew with a sycophantic smile.

"Rainbird," said Lord Guy, "have I missed your performance?"

"No, my lord. I have not had a chance to get started."

"I look forward to seeing it. I suggest you retire belowstairs with Joseph until such time as the room is cleared. Miss Jones, your arm. We will also retire."

Esther blinked up at him. How odd, she thought, to be able actually to look up at a man.

She allowed him to lead her from the room after stopping to give her butler, Graves—who was found hiding in a corner of the hall—instructions for the maids.

The mothers trailed behind.

Back in the drawing-room, Esther waited until the ladies were seated and then asked, rather frostily, "To what do I owe the honour of your visit, my lord?"

"Will you not present me first?" asked Lord Guy, smiling down into her eyes.

"Oh!" Esther blushed and made the introduction: "Lord Guy Carlton—who is presently residing at Number Sixty-seven Clarges Street," she added maliciously, hoping that the name of that house of ill repute would be enough to wipe the smiles off the faces of the ladies.

But all it did was to make them seem more charmed with him than ever. Slyly they teased him about the "goings-on" at that famous party—for the fame of the debauch had spread about the West End. Lord Guy made a moving speech about the bloodiness of war and how it made him behave like any common foot-soldier on leave. They sighed sympathetically and said it was perfectly understandable.

"I fear my lord is a rake," said Esther, impatient with all this hero worship.

"Oh, my dear," tittered the Countess of Resway, once more patronising, "when you become accustomed to tonnish ways, you will find everyone loves a rake!"

"Alas! They cannot love me," said Lord Guy, "for Miss Jones has reformed me."

"I ask you again," said Esther, colouring, "the reason for your visit, my lord."

"I had forgotten the time we were to go driving," said Lord Guy, "and called to refresh my memory. But it was five, was it not?"

There was a little silence. Esther was about to say he was lying, she had never made such an arrangement, when she caught a look of naked, venomous jealousy in the countess's eyes.

A very feminine impulse, immediately regretted, made her say, "Yes, it was five," and then she avoided Lord Guy's amused gaze.

Outside the house, Mr. Roger fidgeted impatiently.

"Your cheroots, sir," said a voice from the pavement.

He looked down and saw Manuel. "How the deuce did you know where to find me?" he demanded.

"I saw milord's carriage leaving just as I was coming back, and I run after it."

Mr. Roger looked at him suspiciously. "Does it usually take you several hours to find cheroots, Manuel?"

"No, sir. But these are the best in London. I go to the City for them."

Mr. Roger had an uneasy feeling that the Spaniard was laughing at him somewhere behind those expressionless eyes of his.

"Cut along home then," he said sharply. "I'll follow you. I think Lord Guy is going to be engaged for some time."

Indoors, Esther was covertly studying Lord Guy as he

sat, very much at his ease, talking to the ladies. She put down her glass of lemonade and poured herself a glass of champagne instead. She felt the need to fortify herself against the time when the party would be over and she would need to tell Lord Guy she had no intention of going driving with him.

Although she had damned him as a rake and libertine, she had to admit to herself she had found him attractive, but had dismissed that attraction as some inherited flaw from her father which made a man of low morals seem appealing. It came as a shock to see these tonnish matrons found him attractive as well. They were beginning to compete quite nastily with each other for his attention, and Esther heaved a sigh of relief when a cleaned and restored Joseph arrived to announce the start of Rainbird's performance.

The children were sitting in rows on the floor, looking chastened and sulky. Lord Guy had cleverly recognised a bully in Bartholomew and knew the unlovely boy would enjoy making them work while doing none of it himself.

The curtains were drawn, and Rainbird stood behind a table at the end of the room with only one oil lamp for illumination.

Chairs for the ladies and Lord Guy were lined up behind the children.

Peter and Amy edged back until they were sitting with their backs to Esther's skirts. "Why did you have to find such awful children?" whispered Peter fiercely, who had not enjoyed being bossed about in his own home by Bartholomew.

Esther quelled him with a frown and glanced covertly at the little gold watch pinned to her bosom. Not long to go and then she could get rid of them all.

Rainbird began his show. The bored audience became

a mildly appreciative one and finally a rapturous one as Rainbird produced coloured balls from ears, a rabbit out of a three-cornered hat, a pigeon from his coat-tails, and then a string of bright handkerchiefs out of his sleeve. While Rainbird proceeded to juggle two plates, one candlestick, and three balls, Joseph left the room and came back with six pine torches. The lamp was put out, the torches were lit, and Rainbird juggled them until they looked like a ring of fire about him. Even Joseph, who had seen Rainbird perform this trick before in the servants' hall at Clarges Street during the long winter evenings, began to cheer and applaud.

Lord Guy watched bemused. *What a very strange butler,* he thought. *Perhaps all servants are amazingly gifted and we never find out because we look on them as necessary appendages to the household, nothing more.*

Rainbird's final trick was to take his three-cornered hat and produce gifts for each child out of it, toy soldiers for the boys, and beautifully carved farm animals for the girls.

Nannies and governesses, who had been summoned by their harassed mistresses during the height of the trouble, but had arrived shortly after Lord Guy to find the battle over, stood waiting in the hall, their faces stern. They knew once they got their charges back to the nursery that their rule would once more be absolute. Parents, they thought, were a necessary evil who hardly saw their offspring from one year's end to another and yet, when they did, spoiled them so badly it took several weeks to bring them to heel again.

The children's mothers departed with many protestations of affection for their "dear Miss Jones."

Rainbird, with Joseph's help, was rapidly bundling up his tricks and would soon leave. Peter and Amy had been taken up to the nursery. Esther knew she was going to be left alone with Lord Guy unless she did something about it quickly. Even the usually attentive Miss Fipps had murmured something about needing to lie down after all the excitement and had drifted off.

"It was all a joke," she said nervously. "Driving . . . us . . . I mean."

"On the contrary," he said, "fetch your bonnet and come with me. It will do your social consequence no harm, Miss Jones."

"It is not that I am not grateful to you," said Esther. "I am. Very. How is it you really happened to arrive at such an opportune moment?"

"I happened to be passing and heard the noise. There is no need to thank me. All you have to do is come driving with me."

"Very well," mumbled Esther ungraciously, thinking that a drive would not take very long, and obviously the easiest way to get rid of him was by consenting to go.

An amused smile curling his lips, Lord Guy watched her ascending the stairs. Then he went outside the house and looked about.

Manuel was standing on the pavement.

"My carriage," said Lord Guy. "If Mr. Roger has taken it, find it and get it back. I want my curricle, not the closed carriage."

"Very good, my lord."

Lord Guy went back inside and settled himself to wait.

After half an hour, Esther came downstairs again, wearing a new carriage dress of sapphire-blue merino edged with velvet. She had a jaunty little shako perched on her pomaded red curls.

Lord Guy bowed. "You look magnificent," he said quietly.

"I am afraid I cannot claim to be intelligent in matters

of dress," said Esther. "I have just recently hired a companion, a Miss Fipps, who is extraordinarily clever in choosing modes. Did you meet Miss Fipps today?"

"Ah, I think I hear my carriage now," said Lord Guy, ignoring the question.

Lord Guy, once they were outside, sent his coachman away, saying he would drive himself. Manuel remained on the backstrap.

"No, Manuel," said Lord Guy. "I do not need you either. Go and help Rainbird carry his things back to Clarges Street."

While Lord Guy helped Esther into his racing curricle and then climbed in and took the reins, two small faces were pressed against the glass of the nursery window, high above them.

"He's taller than she is," said Amy. "That's *very* important."

"You're always dreaming of carrying Esther's train at her wedding," scoffed Peter. "Look at that servant! He *is* sinister. I swear he is a spy. If only we could unmask him!"

"Mr. Rainbird could unmask him," said Amy. "Mr. Rainbird is a magician."

"We'll go and talk to him if he has not left," said Peter. Then his face fell. "But I heard Lord Guy tell Manuel to go into the house and help Rainbird.

"Wait!" hissed Peter. "He is not yet going. He is looking after Esther and Lord Guy with a nasty look on his face."

"Stoopid. How can you see his face from here? I can only see the top of his head."

"The top of his head has a nasty look," said Peter stubbornly. "See! He is not going to help Rainbird. He is walking away. Let's go, Amy, and catch Rainbird before he leaves!"

Rainbird, Joseph, and Angus were gathered in the saloon. "I still think you're trying to take my job," said Esther's butler gloomily. "Miss Jones is always sending for you. 'T ain't natural for a lady to entertain a butler to tea."

"I don't want your stupid job," said Rainbird, who was tired. It had taken a stupendous effort of will to let the children rampage about until Lord Guy's arrival. His livery and Joseph's were stained with cream and jam. They had sponged their clothes as best they could, but they both knew it would take an evening's hard work to get the mess out completely.

"Naebody seems tae appreciate my art," mourned Angus. "Fancy making confections and jellies just for a lot o' bairns to throw about. Michty me! Would ye look at that."

He pointed to the picture of the famous evangelist above the fireplace. Some child had painted a moustache on him and also drawn bullets coming out of the end of his pointing finger so that he looked as if he were in the act of shooting himself in the ear.

"All in a good cause," said Rainbird. He turned and saw Peter and Amy standing at the door, hand in hand.

"The only good children in London," said Rainbird with a smile.

"We cannot understand," said Peter, "why you let them go on so, Mr. Rainbird?"

"Yes, why didn't you turn them all into frogs?" asked Amy.

"It wasn't my day for turning people into frogs," said Rainbird. "Joseph, take the other end of this box, and Angus . . ."

"Oh, *please*, Mr. Rainbird," said Peter, rolling an anguished eye in Graves' direction, "may we help you as well?"

"Esther won't mind," pleaded Amy. "It's only around the corner."

From their rolling eyes and grimaces, Rainbird gathered the children wanted to talk to him alone. It would do no harm to take them along.

"Here," he said, "you can carry this bag of balls, Master Peter. But only as far as Clarges Street, mind! Then one of the maids will take you back."

"And who is this?" asked Mrs. Middleton, when Peter and Amy appeared in the servants' hall.

"May I present Master Peter and Miss Amy Jones," said Rainbird. "I am sure they would like some lemonade."

When the children were seated at the table, Rainbird said, "I have a feeling you want to talk to me about something, Master Peter. What is it?"

"Where is that foreign servant?" asked Peter.

"Gone out, and good riddance," said Jenny.

"Amy and I think he is a spy," said Peter solemnly.

"Indeed," said Rainbird politely. "And what makes you think that?"

"We saw him in the park," said Peter. "He was writing stuff in a book and watching the troops. We crept up on him to see what he was writing but he caught us and shook us and shouted at us. Lord Guy came up then and demanded to see the book. Manuel gave it to him, and Lord Guy glanced at it and then said it seemed to be all right, *but it was the wrong book!* It was a black book, similar to the one he had been writing in, but the one he gave Lord Guy was shiny and new, and the one he had been writing in was worn."

"But he has only to read the newspapers for descriptions of numbers and regiments," said Rainbird.

"That's what Lord Guy said," said Peter, disappointed.

"That's funny," said Lizzie shyly. "I did not tell you, Mr. Rainbird, but the first time I met Miss Jones when she was in Kensington Gardens with the children, I saw Manuel, just as I was leaving. He was watching the troops and writing in a book."

"I said he was a spy then," said Peter gloomily, "but Esther also said he could just read the newspapers."

"Aye, well, maybe that's why there was a hole cut out of the newspaper the other day," put in Angus.

They all looked at him in surprise.

"I'm sure we are imagining things, Master Peter," said Rainbird. He cocked his head to one side and then slid away from the table, walked quietly to the door and flung it open.

Manuel was standing outside.

"Were you listening to us?" demanded Rainbird furiously.

"Me," said the servant contemptuously. "Why should I wish to listen to you?"

He turned and walked away, leaving the servants looking at each other.

Lord Guy was disappointed in his companion. He had pointed out various notables, he had talked of the theatre, he had talked about the success of her party, and all she had answered was curt monosyllables—yes, no, and oh.

He wanted to shrug off the whole idea of courting Miss Jones, but the physical attraction she held for him grew stronger by the minute, and as his impatience with her grew in strength, so did the intense longing to hold her in his arms.

Then a squadron of volunteers who were drilling in

the park raised their rifles and fired a volley. His horses shied and he reined in, jumped down, and spoke to them soothingly until he had quietened them. He climbed back in and took up the reins. "Are you all right?" he asked Esther, and then two things happened at once.

For Lord Guy, Hyde Park receded, to be replaced with a battlefield. Cannon roared, horses screamed, and once again that little drummer boy, Jimmy Watson, barely eleven years of age, stared up at him with pleading, tortured eyes, crying "Shoot me, my lord. I cannot bear the pain." Lord Guy's face turned chalk-white, and he covered his face with his hands.

At the same moment, Esther was looking appalled at a little carriage that had stopped alongside. It was pulled by a pretty milk-white mare and was in charge of a richly dressed brunette. The horse had reared and, like Lord Guy, the brunette had stopped. But the minute her horse was quiet, she started lashing along its flanks with her whip until a long, savage scarlet weal showed where she had cut open its hide.

Esther did not pause to think. She leapt down, marched over, seized the whip out of the girl's hand, and threw it into the bushes.

"You are a *monster!*" she cried.

The girl looked at her haughtily. "I am Lady Penworthy. Who are you?"

"I am Miss Esther Jones, and I take leave to tell you, you are a cruel and unfeeling girl. How dare you treat that inoffensive animal in such a way?"

"John," called Lady Penworthy to her footman on the backstrap. "Fetch my whip."

The footman jumped down. "If you raise that whip again," said Esther, "I shall take it from you and whip *you.*"

The brunette cowered before the fiery blaze in Esther's eyes. "It's a stupid horse," she said sulkily.

"Then you have no further use for it," said Esther. She tugged open her reticule and drew out a large sheaf of banknotes. "You will find a hundred pounds here," said Esther coldly. "I will buy your horse."

Lady Penworthy looked at her in amazement. The horse had cost fifteen guineas. A look of greed shone in her eyes. Jones! Of course, this must be the rich Miss Jones of whom everyone was talking.

The footman came up with the whip.

Esther wrenched it from him and stood like an Amazon. "Well, Lady Penworthy?" she asked.

"Oh, very well," said Lady Penworthy cheerfully. She jumped down lightly and snatched the money. Esther turned to the footman. "Take the mare out of the poles and tie it behind my carriage."

A curious crowd was beginning to gather.

Esther looked at Lord Guy. Why had he not come to her aid? He was sitting very still, his hands over his face. *Probably pretending he isn't here,* thought Esther impatiently.

Arrangements were made for the collection of Lady Penworthy's carriage. Stiffly, Esther, casting a fulminating look in the direction of her silent companion, offered Lady Penworthy a drive home. But, cheerfully waving the sheaf of notes, Lady Penworthy was already heading towards a friend's carriage. She knew she carried with her, not only one hundred pounds, but the best piece of gossip in London.

Esther climbed in beside Lord Guy. The ton stayed to watch, openly and loudly discussing her charms, the gentlemen saying she looked magnificent, and the ladies tittering in a pitying way and saying all that money must have turned her brain. One hundred pounds for such a little mare!

"Do you want me to drive *as well*, sir?" said Esther, between her teeth.

Lord Guy, surrounded by the dead and dying, did not hear.

Esther jerked his hands down from his face and then gazed at him in alarm. His face was deathly white and his eyes fixed in a blind stare.

"Oh, my lord," she cried. "You are ill!" She fished in her reticule, took out a bottle of cologne and a clean handkerchief, and proceeded to bathe his temples. Esther had a very strong maternal instinct. When he shuddered and murmured, "Oh, such death, such suffering. Will it never end?" she knew immediately he was in the grip of a nightmare. Forgetting about the staring, curious crowd, forgetting Lord Guy was a rake and a libertine, she put her arms round him and hugged him as she hugged the children when they had bad dreams and said softly, "Shhh! You are not at war. You are here with Esther. Everything is all right."

Gradually his eyes focussed on the beautiful face so close to his own. In a dazed way, he saw the tenderness in her eyes, he felt the warmth of her bosom and the pressure of her arms. He did not know where he was and he did not care. He wrapped his arms around her and kissed her passionately on the mouth, more passionately than he had ever kissed a woman in the whole of his life. Esther's concern for his welfare was so acute that she did not resist for one little first moment, and that moment was her undoing. She felt her body leap into flame, and if the deafening cheer from the onlookers had not brought her to her senses, she might have begun to kiss him back.

She jerked away, her face flaming, and said between her teeth, "You seem determined to make a vulgar spectacle of me. Drive on!"

Lord Guy looked about him in a startled way, cursed

under his breath, and picked up the reins. He was in despair. About every notable in London society appeared to be on the scene. In even more black despair, he saw the florid features of the Prince of Wales, his corpulent figure perched high in a swan-necked phaeton. Lord Guy bowed, and Esther, her face the colour of beetroot, bowed as well.

"What's going on, heh?" called the Prince.

"Lord Guy Carlton at your service, Your Royal Highness. May you be the first to wish me well. Miss Jones has done me the honour to grant me her hand in marriage."

"Spring in the air, what!" cried the Prince with a jolly laugh. "It's the nesting season, heh. I said, the nesting season."

Everyone about dutifully laughed.

"Invite me to the wedding," said the prince in high good humour. "Can't 'member when I was so entertained."

"We shall be honoured," said Lord Guy easily, "to welcome Your Highness's presence at our marriage ceremony."

"Do not forget," said the Prince. He moved on, and society clicked and urged their mounts as they followed in line behind him.

Esther and Lord Guy were left alone.

"I could not say anything else," he said plaintively. "Miss Jones, you can call it off, but we must send a notice of our engagement to the newspapers."

"Never!" said Esther. "You tricked me. You only pretended to go into a trance to get my sympathy."

"No," said Lord Guy sadly. "I would that were true. It was that volley of shots that affected my brain. I am haunted by nightmares, even during the day. I came out of my nightmare to find you in my arms. The transition from hell to heaven was too fast for me. Miss Jones, you *must* forgive me."

Esther clutched her head. "Oh, the shame of it all!" she cried. "After all my good intentions—to be tied to a rake!"

"You are not tied," he pointed out. "We shall be engaged this week, which will immediately make our scandalous behaviour respectable. Then, having satisfied the morals of society, we can be separated the next. I shall soon be going back to the wars."

"You, my lord, are in no fit state to go to any war."

"What else happened while I was out?" said Lord Guy. "Why, for example, is there a strange and bleeding horse behind my carriage?"

Curtly, Esther explained.

"Then the least I can do is buy the mare from you," he said.

"Fustian," said Esther roundly. "Since you are returning to the wars, you will not be able to look after a horse, let alone a wife."

"Oh, do not make me even more ashamed than I feel," he said quietly.

"What am I to do?" cried Esther. "The Prince of Wales . . ."

"Society will have something else to talk about next week," he said. "An engagement for a week will quieten scandal. You do not want Peter and Amy to suffer because of my behaviour—behaviour, I may point out, which was really no fault of my own. I did not know what I was doing."

"Oh," said Esther bleakly, feeling very sad. Then she rallied with an effort. "One week, then, my lord," she said firmly. "And during that week you will behave like a gentleman. Do I make myself clear?"

"Yes, ma'am," said Lord Guy meekly. He picked up the reins and turned his head away so that Esther should not see the triumphant smile on his face.

Chapter Seven

"Morning Post" ("The Times" won't trust me),
  help me, as I know you can;
I will pen an advertisement—that's a never-failing
  plan.

"WANTED—By a bard in wedlock, some interesting
  young woman:
"Looks are not so much an object, if the shiners be
  forthcoming!

"Hymen's chains," the advertiser vows, "shall be
  but silken fetters,
"Please address to A.T., Chelsea. N.B.—You must
  pay the letters."

—SIR THEODORE MARTIN

"What has our Lizzie been up to?" asked Rainbird as Mrs. Middleton dragged the blushing scullery maid into the servants' hall.

"Our Lizzie has a letter and refuses to let me see it," said the housekeeper.

"Now, Lizzie," said Rainbird, "girls in your position

are not supposed to receive letters without telling their betters where they come from. You don't have any family, so who has been writing to you?"

"It's private, Mr. Rainbird, sir," said Lizzie desperately.

Rainbird felt uncomfortable. Mrs. Middleton was right, of course. On the other hand, it did seem terrible that Lizzie was forbidden any private life at all.

"Let her keep it," said Alice slowly. "Seems to me we do have some rights. Lizzie wouldn't do anything wrong."

"She's bin writing for jobs, that's what," cried Dave. "You shouldn't ha' taught 'er to write."

"You haven't, have you, Lizzie?" asked Rainbird.

"Not a job, no," whispered Lizzie.

"Here comes that Manuel," called Joseph.

"I'll speak to you later, Lizzie," said Rainbird. The staff were united in their dislike of Lord Guy's servant and never discussed anything personal in front of him.

"That ees that," said Manuel furiously.

"What ees what?" mocked Jenny.

"My lord tell me to go to the *Times* and put an advertisement in to say he wed this Miss Jones."

They all cheered, and Manuel looked at them angrily. "It mean he no' go back to Spain. I rot here in this stinking country."

"Watch your mouth," said Rainbird. "If you've been told to put in an advertisement, go and do it, and don't stand around here sulking and glooming. Off with you."

"One day, you be sorry you speak to Manuel with disrespect," said the servant, charging out.

"Good," said Rainbird. "I'll say one thing for that Spanish onion, he don't stay around very long, always creeping here and there."

"What do you say to this idea?" said Angus MacGregor.

"We wait until he's asleep tonight and take a look in his wee book. He must keep it on him, for I searched his stuff and it wasnae there."

Mrs. Middleton let out a squawk. "You are not taking those children seriously, Mr. MacGregor?"

"Aye, I am a wee bit. I hae a mind to make sure."

The men fell to discussing ways to stay awake to search Manuel's clothes when he fell asleep. Lizzie began to edge away towards the door.

"No, Lizzie," said Rainbird, his quick eye catching the movement. "Come here. I am afraid we are going to have to see that letter."

Tears started to Lizzie's eyes as she reluctantly handed it over.

Rainbird read it aloud. "Dear Miss L. O'B," he read. "In answer to your advertisement in the *Morning Post,* I am a single fellow of comfortable means and I feel we should suit. I am not ill-favoured and have a cobbler's stall at the corner of St. Paul's churchyard. If you call, we can discuss matters to our mutual benefit. Yr Humble Servant, Josiah Dancer."

"Goodness!" said Alice, round-eyed. "Our Lizzie has gone and advertised for a husband. Why, Lizzie?"

"I don't want to be a servant anymore," said Lizzie, twisting her apron in her work-worn fingers.

"But we only need about two more Seasons," cried Rainbird, "and then we can have that pub, and you will be independent."

"But never really, please, Mr. Rainbird, sir," said Lizzie. "You see, we'll all keep our ranks, I know we will. You and Mrs. Middleton will be in charge; Mr. MacGregor will cook; Joseph, Alice, and Jenny will wait; Dave will do the pots; and I will be the scullery maid, just like always."

"No, Lizzie," said Rainbird, "we will hire a couple of

servants for the heavy work. You will be an independent lady."

"I want to use my share of the Vail Box for a dowry," said Lizzie, drying her tears with a corner of her apron. "I want a home of my own."

"Did you give this address to the newspaper?" asked Rainbird.

"No," said Lizzie. "I collected the reply. There was only the one."

"Come on, Liz," wheedled Joseph. "You can't leave us. Look, I got you a present." He drew the red silk rose out of his pocket and held it out. Lizzie winced and turned away. She recognised that rose, the rose given to Miss Hunt, the rose which had nearly broken her heart and had made her spend most of her precious bonus of two pounds putting an advertisement in the *Post*.

"I don't want it," she said, putting her hands behind her back. "It was for Miss Hunt."

"I really bought it for you. Honest, I did," said Joseph. "Luke was there, and I couldn't tell him it was for a scullery maid, so I lied and said it was for that Miss Hunt. Luke made me try to give it to her."

"I want permission to go out, Mr. Rainbird," said Lizzie in a shaky voice. "I'll always be the scullery maid here, and even Joseph is ashamed of me. Mr. Dancer sounds nice and he's literate."

"Lizzie, Lizzie. He paid someone to write that for him."

"I want to go," said Lizzie, stamping her foot.

"Know your place, Lizzie," said Mrs. Middleton, "and don't ever speak to Mr. Rainbird like that again."

"Oh, leave her," said Rainbird wearily. "Go on, Lizzie, 'fore my lord gets back and starts ringing the bells and makes me change my mind. We'll manage without you for a little."

When Lizzie had left, they all looked reproachfully at Joseph.

The front-parlour bell began to ring, and Rainbird ran to answer it.

Lord Guy and Mr. Roger were sitting together. "Bring us a bottle of the best burgundy, Rainbird," said Lord Guy.

"Certainly, my lord," said Rainbird, "and allow me to offer you my congratulations."

"Thank you, but your congratulations are not in order. Miss Jones became engaged to me because I involved her in a scene before the Prince of Wales and had to propose to her to save her reputation. She plans to terminate the engagement in a week."

"All sorts of things can happen in a week," said Mr. Roger bracingly.

"I received a note from Miss Fipps that they are to go to the opera tonight," said Lord Guy. "I hope some fool does not let off a squib or I might go into a trance again. What a milksop I am! London's full of fighting men who don't faint and turn green at the memory of battle. *You* don't, Tommy."

"Doesn't affect me that way," said Mr. Roger with a shrug, "but I get some devilish nightmares."

"But nonetheless, Rainbird," said Lord Guy, "I am indebted to you for the idea of the children's party."

"I felt sure it would provide you with an opportunity to appear in a good light, my lord," said Rainbird.

"There is that," said Lord Guy. "It was also enough to put me right off any idea of setting up my own nursery. Bring that bottle, Rainbird, and then tell Manuel I need him to help me dress."

"I believe he has stepped out, my lord."

"Then send someone to find him. I really must think seriously about sending Manuel home. He has turned most odd since his arrival in England."

Lizzie walked all the way to the City, anger with Joseph speeding her steps. Dancer was a happy-sounding name, she thought. He had his own stall, therefore he was independent. Through him, she could escape her basement life, a life where she was not allowed to marry. Even if they got the pub, Joseph would never ask her to marry him. He would always think of her as a scullery maid.

Evening was falling, and fog was beginning to creep up from the river. She crossed the Fleet Bridge where nuts, gingerbread, oranges, and oysters lay piled up in movable shops. Saloop stalls were dotted at the corners of the winding City streets. The saloop stall was a small kitchen table on wheels, with cupboards, and fitted with an urn for the making of the saloop—an infusion of sassafras, sugar, and milk, sold at three halfpence a bowl. Its price made it popular with workers, who found the price of tea and coffee too high.

One of the Prime Bits of Gig of the all-night Bucks, successors to the Mohocks, was to overturn these stalls and wreck the owners' livelihood. But it was not only the loutish members of the aristocracy who put decent folks in danger. The lower orders had been getting uppity ever since the French Revolution and were just as happy to molest a respectable female or throw an elderly gentleman in the kennel.

Lizzie had learned to keep a weather eye out for trouble. With her hair covered with her shawl, she hurried on up Ludgate Hill.

But before she could reach St. Paul's, she had to crouch back against the houses to let a crowd of dustmen go by. One dustman was being subjected to Burning Shame, having been found in bed with another dustman's wife, and tried in a City tavern. His hat was decorated with a crown of holly and two large carrots. He was mounted on the shoulders of four dustmen, and a procession was formed, with the chief dustman leading it, and another, with a bell, announcing the crime. Then came the rest of the dustmen, wearing their fantail hats, each decorated with holly and a lighted candle. Behind rode the mounted culprit, considerately provided with a pot of beer and a pipe, and the rear of the procession was made up of the dustmen's wives and daughters.

Lizzie backed into a dark doorway, not out of fear of the people in the procession, but because she did not have any money with her. The dustmen with boxes were collecting money on either side of the street. When they considered they had enough, then the whole crowd, including the culprit and the wronged husband, would settle down for a whole night's drinking in one of the taverns.

When the last candlelit hat had bobbed past down Ludgate Hill, she hurried on. The fog was thickening and taking on that greyish-yellowish hue that meant it was going to become a suffocating pea-souper.

By the time she reached St. Paul's churchyard, she was anxious to have the meeting over and done with so that she could return to Clarges Street while she could still see her way.

She hesitated a little all the same, overcome with shyness, peering through the fog at the row of little stalls like medieaval booths, lined up against the churchyard railings.

She saw the cobbler's stall. There was a young man in front of it. He was well set up, with broad shoulders, lean hips, and good legs. His hair was tied back at the nape of his neck.

Lizzie took a deep breath and started forward.

"Lizzie!" A hand caught her arm.

In a fright, she wrenched her arm away, and then found herself looking up into Joseph's round blue eyes.

"Don't do it, Liz," he said.

"I shall do as I please," said Lizzie, made heady with power. What a weakling Joseph now seemed compared to that strong young man. Joseph was out of his livery. He was wearing a suit of ordinary brown wool with a coarse cotton shirt and a belcher neckerchief.

The sight of an ordinary Joseph—no longer flattered by black-and-gold livery—strengthened Lizzie's resolve.

"Leave me be," she said. With head held high, she walked toward the cobbler's stall.

But as she approached, the young man walked away along by the churchyard, whistling to himself. Lizzie watched him go, and stood irresolute. He had been only a passer-by.

"Lizzie," came Joseph's voice in her ear again.

"Leave me alone, Joseph, do," said Lizzie, but in less determined tones than she had used before. "I came to see this Mr. Dancer, and see him I will!"

"Well, let me come with you, just to make sure he's honest," said Joseph.

Lizzie looked about. The fog was getting thicker. A drunk reeled past, staggered, and swore.

"All right, then," said Lizzie, "but you're not to interfere."

Together they approached the stall. A wizened little man popped out from the back and looked up at them curiously.

"Mr. Dancer?" asked Lizzie timidly, thinking this might be the father.

"Not me," said the man. "Minding 'is stall for 'im. Be back soon. You wantin' 'im?"

"Yes," said Lizzie.

"See 'ere. I wants to go for a pint o' shrub. Keep an eye on the place. Be back in a tick."

Without waiting for a reply, he scuttled off into the fog.

"Let's go, Liz," wheedled Joseph.

"No," said Lizzie. Somehow, she was sure Mr. Dancer would turn out to be someone like the young man she had seen, someone to be proud of, someone to keep house for.

They waited uneasily while the fog thickened. Lizzie could barely see Joseph's face.

Night had fallen. The fog had silenced everything. Carriage wheels were muffled. Passers-by loomed up as blacker blobs in the gloom and then disappeared. Lizzie shivered and drew her shawl more tightly about her.

"Someone's coming," said Joseph, "and I think I heard the name Dancer."

Suddenly, unnaturally loud in the fog, a woman's voice said, "I hopes you know what you're a doing of, Mr. Dancer. Wot if the law gets you? What'll become of me and the childer?"

"I'm a careful man, Mrs. Dancer, that you should know by now" was the guttural reply. "If this Miss L. O'B turns up, I tells her I've got to see the dowry first. She brings it over. We takes it from her. The law won't bother wiff silly girls wot advertises in the papers. Jeff Barker over in Cheapside had fifty pound off of a girl wiff the same trick."

"She'd better show up," came the woman's voice. "You paid a crown to the scrivener for that letter. A whole crown!"

Joseph slid an arm around Lizzie's waist and led her unresistingly away.

He did not say anything, simply walked along slowly, holding her, until he felt she was crying, and stopped, and put his arms about her, holding her close and letting her cry.

At last, when he felt she was becoming calmer, he said, "I've got money, Lizzie. We'll have something strong to make us feel better and then we'll get home somehow."

"It's not home," said Lizzie bitterly. "How can sixty-seven Clarges Street be home?"

Joseph wanted to say because that was the place where everyone loved her and cared about her, but pride stopped him.

"Here's a tavern," he said instead. He guided her through the door, noticing with relief it was a respectable establishment.

"Eh, say, wehtter," said Joseph, genteel once more, "we'll hehve two glesses of rum."

"Right you are, guv," said the waiter cheerily. "Bad night for you and the missus to be out."

"Yes," said Joseph. He sat beside Lizzie on a settle near the fire and took her hand. He wondered all at once what it would be like to be married to someone like Lizzie, to have a real home, not to be constantly at someone's beck and call, not to be tied by fetters of class that bit like iron.

"Luke said the other day as how you was getting to look uncommon pretty," said Joseph.

"Did he?" said Lizzie. She tried to shrug off the compliment, but a warm glow started somewhere in the pit of her stomach and spread up through her whole body.

"Yes, he did. He thought I was interested in that awful frump, Miss Hunt, and he said I'd be better off with you because you'd turned into a looker," said Joseph, and seized with a fit of mad daring, he squeezed Lizzie's hand.

The waiter put two glasses of rum and a jug of hot

water in front of them and sauntered off to tell the other waiter to go have a look at the little lady over at the fire who looked like one of them mad-oneys in the Bible pictures.

"My dear Miss Jones," ventured Miss Fipps, "I really do not think we should venture out this evening."

"It's just a little mist," said Esther, letting the curtain fall back.

"You know how dirty fog can make everything," pursued Miss Fipps in her gentle but stubborn way. "Your new opera gown will be quite ruined."

"I can put my cloak right round it," said Esther, feeling petulant and impatient, and immediately ashamed of her childish thoughts. Miss Fipps was being eminently sensible. She, Esther, would normally have been equally as sensible, but she had never worn such a gown before or gone to the opera. Her gown was of gold tissue, a miracle of the dressmaker's art. Esther had felt like quite another person when she had looked at herself in the looking-glass. If she did not go to the opera, then . . . no one . . . would see it. She voiced that thought aloud.

"Of what is the use, Miss Fipps," she said, "of paying a vast price for a box at the opera and wearing grand clothes if no one is going to see the clothes and the box is not going to be used?"

"We can go tomorrow night," pointed out the infuriating Miss Fipps.

"No, I feel I must go," said Esther. "I should at least appear in public with my supposed fiancé after that scandal."

"As you wish," said Miss Fipps. "My own gown has seen better days, so it does not matter if it is ruined."

"As to that," said Esther, looking at Miss Fipps' depressing round gown of purple silk, "I think you should feel free to order what you want from my dressmaker."

"You already pay me a very good salary," said Miss Fipps comfortably. "Such excitement. I have never been *paid* before."

"How did you exist?" asked Esther, realising again she knew very little about her companion.

"I have quite a number of rich relatives," said Miss Fipps. "I am normally passed from one to the other."

"How depressing! Which relative did you come to London to stay with?"

But, as sometimes happened, Miss Fipps appeared to become unaccountably deaf.

"If we are going," she said, "we may as well have the carriage brought around. That is, if you do not mind being unfashionable and want to see the whole performance."

"Why is it unfashionable? What other reason is there for going to the opera?"

"To see and be seen. To go to the ball and supper afterwards. To make suitable connections for the coming Season."

"I wish to be unfashionable, Miss Fipps. If you do not mind, I would like to go now."

Miss Fipps nodded in a vague way and rang the bell to order the carriage.

She was an odd woman, reflected Esther. She appeared fat and vague and timid and kept much in the background, but she was somehow always there when needed, and had a practical way of checking dressmaker's bills and knowing which shops sold the best feathers and materials. She was also very good with the servants and had a quick eye to notice when a housemaid had a toothache or whether a footman was worried about some personal matter. Hitherto, Esther had considered herself a good mistress, but she had never before thought of servants as being people to be particularly concerned about unless they actually voiced their complaints and worries. She considered she was doing her duty if they were well dressed and well fed and if everything to further their education and Bible studies had been attended to. That servants had loves and passions, griefs, and the toothache, just like their masters, was a new idea. She supposed Miss Fipps' life as a poor relation where one was, after all, a kind of servant, subject to the whims of the richer relative, had given her an added insight, and in this Esther was right. It was an age when people firmly believed that God put one in one's appointed station, and to sulk or be discontented in it was going against the will of God. In many ways, this belief protected the servants from envying their betters, and their betters from troubling themselves about what went on in their servants' minds.

But she had further reason to speculate about her companion's background as their carriage crawled inch by inch through the now suffocating fog in the direction of Covent Garden. London was lost, swimming in a thick sea of fog. Beyond the carriage window there was black nothingness.

"Dear me," said Miss Fipps, rubbing the glass of the carriage window with an edge of her stole, "I wonder if Carlton will venture out in such weather."

"Carlton?" said Esther sharply. "Do you mean Lord Guy?"

"Yes, Miss Jones."

"Did you know him before?"

The carriage gave a lurch, and Esther was thrown forward. The trap in the roof was raised, and the coachman called down apologetically, "Hit the kerb, ma'am. Can't see a thing in this fog."

"Take your time," called Esther.

The carriage lurched on. After a time, Esther realised Miss Fipps had not answered her question. "Miss Fipps," she said.

The fog was inside the carriage now, and Miss Fipps' face was only a vague white blur under the dim light of the carriage lamp.

"Miss Fipps!" called Esther again.

This time a gentle snore was the only reply.

Esther tucked away that use of Lord Guy's name—Carlton—in the back of her mind, and then her thoughts turned to her little brother and sister. She had not explained to them that the engagement was only for a week, but she had been taken aback by their joy in the news of her engagement. Lord Guy, from the moment he had appeared on the stage at Astley's, had been a hero to them. He was good fun, for had he not aided and abetted Esther in her theatrical performance? He was majestic. Had he not quelled a roomful of hooligans? The fact that Esther had saved the little white mare, whom the children now called Snowball, from further ill treatment appeared to have been forgotten. It was Lord Guy who had brought Snowball home and had actually gone round to the mews and attended to the animal with his own hands. It was Lord Guy who had suggested Snowball would make an excellent mount for the children. Esther did not have the heart to tell them that their hero's morals were of the worst. She decided she must plan a special treat for them on the day she announced the end of her engagement.

Rainbird would know what to do, she thought. Rainbird had risen out of the anonymous mass of London servants to become a special personality in Esther's eyes. She longed to employ him as her own butler, but Graves was a good man and Esther could not bring herself to displace her butler in an age when servants' jobs were notoriously hard to find. Perhaps she could invent another title for Rainbird, Controller of the Household, or something like that, which would establish him in Berkeley Square and have him constantly on hand to advise her.

Other women might dream of a husband to take over the worries of making household decisions and the bringing up of two small children, but Esther did not intend to marry.

And yet the romances she had read had filled her with strange yearnings, even as she laughed at the ridiculous stories.

There was another jolt, and the carriage came to a halt.

"We're here, ma'am," called the coachman.

The footman opened the carriage door and let down the steps. Miss Fipps came awake and peered out into the fog.

"It is very quiet, Miss Jones," she said. "Perhaps the performance has been cancelled."

But Esther could not believe such a thing could happen, not on her first night, not when she was wearing this splendid gown that . . . someone . . . must see.

"Wait here a moment, Miss Fipps," she said.

"Much better to let the footman find out for you," said Miss Fipps. "These terrible fogs can make you lose your way after you have only gone a few paces."

But Esther had had enough of inactivity.

She stepped down into the fog.

"Mama!" wailed a plaintive voice nearby. "Mama!"

"Best get back in the carriage, ma'am," came her footman's voice. "Looks like the theatre's closed."

"How can you *see* if the theatre's even there, let alone tell if it is closed?" said Esther testily. "Oh, wait here, John, until I find out what ails that child."

John, the footman, wanted to protest but was too much in awe of his strong-willed mistress to say anything.

"Mama!" came the child's voice again.

Esther hugged her cloak tightly about her and made her way towards the voice. She practically bumped into a small figure. Bending down, Esther tried to see the child, but between the darkness, for night had fallen, and the thick, all-encompassing fog, she could only make out a dim little shape.

"Where did you last see your mother?" she asked. "Do not cry. I shall find her."

"We came to the opera with Mama," said the child. "We were not to stay for the performance. Our nursemaid was to take us home, that is me and my sister, Louise. I ran away a little from the carriage as a joke. I heard Mama calling that the theatre was closed and I was to come back. I went a little away, just for fun. I-I g-got l-lost."

"Don't cry again," said Esther. "Here! Give me your hand." She fumbled until she felt the child's hand and grasped it firmly.

"Jane!" came a faint voice over to the left. And, immediately after, "Miss Jones," called Miss Fipps' voice over on the right.

"I shall return shortly, Miss Fipps," called Esther, and to the child, "Is your name Jane?"

"Yes."

"Then I think I hear your mother. Come along." And, holding the child's hand, Esther walked off to the left.

"Jane!" sounded the voice, much nearer and clearer. "She is safe with me," called Esther. "Keep calling so that I can find you."

The voice obediently kept calling, but Esther almost bumped into a carriage before she realised she had at last found the child's mother.

108

Although the carriage lamps were burning, they were only two yellow blurs, unable to pierce the fog. Esther handed over the child she had never seen to a mother she could not see either, gracefully accepted effusive thanks, and backed off into the fog to find her own carriage. It was simply a matter of returning the way she had come.

After she had been walking for some time, tracing and retracing her steps, she found she was completely lost—lost in one of London's worst fogs, where sinister figures loomed up out of the thick black clouds and disappeared again like phantoms.

"Miss Fipps!" she called, loudly and sharply.

"Miss Fipps!" mocked a man's coarse voice.

Calling and calling, and tormented by ghostly voices mocking her and echoing her, Esther blundered on through the fog, feeling more and more frightened. She was wearing a particularly fine gold-and-emerald necklace, the first piece of expensive jewellery she had ever treated herself to. She was richly dressed.

She began talking to herself, calling herself to order, telling herself not to panic. A hand seized her cloak and with a little scream of terror, she beat it off. Then another hand grabbed out of the fog, and again she beat it off. She felt the hands were like flames, licking at her clothes, as she smacked and beat at them to escape their clutches.

At last, more frightened than she had ever been in her life before, Esther threw back her head and screamed, "Help! Help me. I am being attacked. Help!"

Silence.

Absolute silence surrounded her. Blackness. But the silence had a waiting quality, as if her unseen tormentors were holding their breath to see if there came any answering call from the watch.

And then, faint and far off, she heard an answering call: "Keep shouting. I am coming."

Sending up a prayer that the voice should prove to belong to a rescuer and not some clever thief, Esther called, "Here. I am here. Over here."

"Keep calling," shouted the voice, nearer now. "And don't move."

"Help. Help me! Here. Over here!" shouted Esther.

"Got you, thank God" came a voice suddenly in her ear, and a strong pair of arms went about her.

"NO!" screamed Esther, now afraid of rape. "Help!"

"My dear Miss Jones, it is I, Carlton. You are safe."

"Carlton?" said Esther weakly. "Oh, Lord Guy, is it indeed you?"

"It is indeed I." He held her in a comforting way, and Esther, feeling as weak and helpless as a child, put her head on his shoulder and began to cry.

"You poor little angel," he said caressingly, and the hitherto independent Miss Esther Jones, all five feet eleven inches of her, put her arms around him and hugged him back, feeling safe at last.

Chapter Eight

In town let me live then, in town let me die,
For in truth, I can't relish the country, not I,
If one must have a villa in summer to dwell,
O, give me the sweet shady side of Pall Mall.

—CHARLES MORRIS

"What a terrible night!" said Rainbird. "I hope Joseph managed to find Lizzie. I don't like to think of any young girl wandering about in this fog. And there's my lord gone out, too. That's the bell. He must be back."

Rainbird darted up the backstairs from the servants' hall and entered the front parlour. But it was only Mr. Roger, calling for another bottle.

"Wonder where Lord Guy is," said Mr. Roger. "It's curst dull sitting here alone. I told him the opera wouldn't be performed tonight, but he insisted on going in case Miss Jones might have had the same idea. Love is a wonderful thing, Rainbird."

"Yes, sir," said Rainbird politely. "You have not yet dined, Mr. Roger, and the hour is getting late. Shall I tell MacGregor to prepare a supper?"

"Yes. No. I don't know. Demne, forget that other bottle. I'll walk round to the club. Can surely find my way to St. James' Street. If Lord Guy comes back, tell him to join me."

"Yes, sir. Will that be White's or Brooks's?"

"White's, of course," said the Tory Mr. Roger. Brooks' was for the Whigs.

After ascertaining that Mr. Roger really meant to walk, Rainbird returned downstairs and asked Jenny and Alice to help him fill up the coal scuttles in the bedrooms. It was going to be a cold night. He heaved a sigh of relief as the kitchen door opened and Joseph and Lizzie came in, hand in hand.

Once the fires had been made up, the beds turned down, and fresh water put in the cans on the toilet tables, the servants returned to their hall and settled down to a late supper. Manuel slid in and took his place at the end of the table. He ate quickly and silently.

"Care for a glass of brandy, Manuel?" asked Rainbird, winking at Angus MacGregor.

"Yes," said the Spanish servant ungraciously.

MacGregor, gathering that Rainbird wished to get the Spaniard drunk, poured him a large measure. Silence fell on the servants. Once the meal was over, Mrs. Middleton retired to her parlour on the half-landing on the backstairs, Jenny and Alice took out sheets and began to mend them, and Lizzie cleared away the dishes and took them through to the scullery to wash. Dave, the pot boy, who had his nose in a Gothic horror story, had to be cuffed and ordered to help her.

Angus MacGregor sat next to Manuel and kept refilling the servant's glass every time he emptied it.

"These will need to be washed when we've finished," sighed Jenny, putting delicate little stitches into a tear in the sheet spread on her lap. Alice nodded. "Terrible bad, this fog," she said in her slow, warm voice. Fog lay in bands of yellowish-grey across the kitchen. "It does dirty everything so. Reckon I don't know why folks live in Town if they don't have to. That Miss Jones now. All that money and yet she lives the year round in Berkeley Square. Can't be good for the children. Do you have fogs like this in Spain, Manuel?"

"No," said Manuel, drinking brandy steadily.

"Got no conversation," said Jenny. "Most servants enjoy a chance to have a bit of a gossip. But not you, Manuel. No, yes, no, yes."

"My Engleesh, she is not good," volunteered Manuel sulkily.

"Now, there's an odd thing," said Alice, putting down her needle. "Sometimes you sound like them Spaniards at the playhouse—I mean when someone English pretends to be Spanish—and then sometimes your English is as good as my lord's."

"I go," said Manuel, getting to his feet and hanging on to the table for support.

He lurched to the door and then could be heard stumbling up the stairs.

"What did you say that for?" said Rainbird angrily. "Angus and me were trying to get him drunk so that when he passed out we could search him."

"Wait a bit," said Alice placidly. "He's gone to his room, and from the look of him he won't stay awake long. Ain't it quiet? You would think the whole of London was dead. Not even a carriage passing. I wonder if my lord found Miss Jones."

"You had wandered quite a way from the theatre, Miss Jones," Lord Guy was saying as he walked along beside her, keeping her arm firmly tucked in his.

"I must apologise for my behaviour," said Esther

stiffly. "I am not in the way of hugging strangers. I was overset."

"Of course you were," he said soothingly. "But we are hardly strangers now. And we *are* engaged to be married."

"Only for a week," said Esther firmly.

"Since you plan to go about in society, you will no doubt be asked why you found me unsuitable. What reason are you going to give?"

"I do not need to give a reason," said Esther. "The world will simply think I have come to my senses. You are a well-known rake."

"On the contrary—I gave one wild party. . . ."

"And *such* a party. That was enough to ruin anyone's reputation."

"Not a member of the peerage," said Lord Guy. "Society will forgive me all, particularly when they see how well you have reformed me."

"Rakes never reform," said Esther.

"What gives you such knowledge of the breed?"

"My father led my mother a most unhappy life."

"Ah, but perhaps he *became* a rake after marriage. Now, I have *been* a rake. That is a different thing entirely. I am determined to marry you, Miss Jones. I may not have made that point clear."

"Why?"

"Because, like all my breed, I am mercenary. I believe you have a rare talent for making money on 'Change. I would avail myself of such a talent."

"That is what I expect of you," sighed Esther. "You may avail yourself of my services, my lord, without having to marry me."

"Of course, there *are* other things."

"Such as?" asked Esther drily.

"Your hair is like fire, your eyes are the eyes of a witch,

your figure excites my senses, and you have an odd tough-
ness of mind which stimulates my own. Furthermore, I love
you. Shall I go on?"

"No. Enough. I do not believe a word of it," cried
Esther, shocked because her treacherous body was reacting
physically to his words as if he had caressed her. "Where
are we going, my lord? We appear to be wandering aim-
lessly."

"I have not the faintest idea where we are," he said
easily.

"Oh, I have been following you blindly. Poor Miss
Fipps. She must be mad with worry."

"Not she. I came across her and your servants outside
the theatre. I told her to be easy in her mind as I was sure
I would find you. I told her to wait for half an hour and then
return to Berkeley Square. She is not as strong as she
appears."

"You *do* know her," said Esther. "You have known her
before. I see it all now. Deceitful Rainbird. And I so grateful
to him for having provided me with a companion at such
short notice. She is one of *your* poor relations!"

"She is my cousin."

"And you foisted her on me!"

"Come, my excellent and sensible Miss Jones. I would
not have you companioned by any silly woman. I care for
you."

"It also saved you from having a poor relation in *your*
own household."

"True."

"Miss Fipps may leave tonight."

"Why? She seems to fill the post excellently. And
would you deny that she has an affection for you?"

"How can I tell?" said Esther wretchedly. "You have

been plotting and scheming behind my back. I know what it is! You do not have any money."

"On the contrary, I am very rich."

"Why don't you leave me alone?"

"Alas, I cannot."

"You want me to stay alive, I presume. Then . . . GET ME HOME!"

"You are shivering," said Lord Guy. "It is quite amazing how a spleenish temper can reduce one's temperature."

"I am *not* in a temper," said Esther. "I want to get out of this fog."

"And so you shall. We shall repair to some tavern or coffee-house and find out where we are."

Esther tried to see his face, but the fog was so thick, she found it was like being blind.

"Are you *sure* you do not know the way?" she asked.

"On my honour. There are sounds coming from the left. Let us go that way."

A dim blur of light suddenly appeared a few inches before their eyes.

"In here," he said.

Esther drew back. "I cannot go into a common tavern, my lord."

"Then let us hope it is an uncommon one, for I cannot walk around in this fog much longer."

Lord Guy ushered Esther into a dark, foggy taproom. There were two men sitting in a corner, half asleep, but apart from them, there were no other customers.

They sat side by side on a settle in front of the fire. The landlord came bustling up. "Where are we?" asked Lord Guy.

"You're in George Yard, sir, off of Long Acre, sir."

"Oh, we *have* wandered. Fetch me the ingredients for a punch."

"I would prefer lemonade," said Esther after a few moments' silence.

"Punch will warm you," he said.

"Punch might make me drunk."

"That I should like to see—the disintegration of the stony-faced Miss Jones."

"I am not stony-faced!"

"Yes, you are. Quite like a statue, down to the smear of soot on your nose."

Esther gave an exclamation of distress. She pulled a steel mirror out of her reticule and dabbed at her nose with a handkerchief.

"Here. Allow me," he said softly. He took the handkerchief from her hand and put a finger under her chin and tilted her face up. He rubbed at the spot of soot, and smiled down into her wide eyes. Her lips, he noticed, were very soft and pink. He remembered how they had felt when he had kissed her in the Park. That memory gleamed in his eyes, and Esther jerked her head away as the landlord came up carrying a tray with two lemons, half a pint of rum, half a pint of brandy, a quarter of a pound of sugar, half a teaspoon of nutmeg, and a kettle of hot water and a large bowl.

"Would you like me to prepare it?" he asked, but Lord Guy waved him away.

Esther watched him prepare the punch, first rubbing the sugar loaves over the rind of the lemons until they were yellow. He appeared completely absorbed in his task. She noticed again the mocking droop to his eyelids and the humorous twist to his mouth, the aristocratic nose, and the glint of his golden hair. Although he looked remarkably clean and fresh, as if he had come straight from the hands of his valet rather than out of a London fog, she persuaded herself he had a shop-soiled, *used* look. No one could live the life he had led without that life corrupting his very soul. Her lip curled in distaste, and then she found he was looking at her curiously.

"You sit there, making me feel like a piece of rotting meat," he said. "Have I such a bad smell?"

"I was thinking of your immortal soul, my lord."

"To err is human, to forgive divine, Miss Jones, or had you forgotten?"

She compressed her lips into a disapproving line and did not reply.

He finished preparing the punch and handed her a glass. Esther sipped it cautiously, but it tasted sweet and tangy and remarkably innocuous.

"Why do you persist in living in Town?" he asked.

"I do not like the country."

"Why, pray?"

"What a lot of questions you do ask," sighed Esther as he refilled her glass. "I like the Town because it is ordered and tame. One can remain anonymous. In the country, everyone gossips and everyone knows one's business."

"You will find, as you mean to join the ranks of society, that people here gossip much more. You see, they have nothing else to do. They watch each other the whole time, searching for scandal, searching for weak spots in the social armour. But I would have thought the children might have benefitted from country air. Have you never even taken them to Brighton?"

"No, my lord."

"You cannot go on forever inflicting your fears on your little brother and sister. They should have the company of other children. . . ."

"Like those monsters at the children's party?"

"Those monsters were with their mamas. With their

tutors and governesses, you will find them quite different. And Peter should have a tutor. Can he ride or fish or hunt?"

"There is no need to do any of these things in London."

"I wish someone would tell that to the Berkeley Hunt." Lord Guy laughed. "They hunt up to the very walls of Kensington Palace, crashing their way through gardens and cucumber frames after a bag fox."

"Peter is being taught to ride Snowball, that little mare I rescued in the Park while you, my lord, were in a trance. Do you really think I ought to drink any more of this stuff?"

"Yes. I apologise for my fit in the Park. It seems I have only to hear or see anything which reminds me of battle and I find myself whirled back among the dead and dying."

"But surely you need not fear the sights and sounds of war anymore," said Esther.

He looked puzzled. "You mean I shall become hardened like a proper soldier?"

"I mean you will not be returning to the wars. . . ."

"On the contrary, my love. I have every intention of going back to take up my command as soon as our honeymoon is over."

"Ah, so you are like all other men. You would marry for the sake of a nursery and then leave your wife while you lead an entirely separate life."

"I had hoped you would come with me. Wellington will not stay in Portugal forever. We will soon be in Spain."

Esther stared at him, round-eyed.

"It is not unusual," he said. "Many men have their wives with them."

"If you loved me, you would not expose me to danger."

"I would not expect you to join me in the front lines, my amazon."

"And what of Peter and Amy?"

"Peter would go to school—which would delight him. Amy would go to my father's with Miss Fipps, where she would play all day long with all my little nieces and nephews."

"But we hardly know each other, and yet you have everything planned."

"Love activates the brain wonderfully."

"Do not talk fustian. What of my stocks and shares?"

"You have enough money, my greedy darling. You will not need very much in the army. Say I am not successful in dragging you to the altar, what will your life be like?"

"Much the same," said Esther. "Ordered and comfortable and—"

"Dull. Oh, so dull. You cannot keep turning to a strange butler for help."

"I intend to offer Rainbird a post in my household."

"But will he take it? He has responsibilities. I tell you, Miss Jones, that is not a staff of servants I have at Clarges Street. That is a tribe, and Rainbird is the headman. If you can imagine them all dressed in beads and feathers and carrying spears, you might be able to understand them better."

Esther did not know quite how it happened, but suddenly the idea of the servants dressed as primitive savages struck her as exquisitely funny. She threw back her head and laughed, her cloak sliding from her shoulders to show the magnificence of her gown and emerald necklace.

The two men who had been sitting in the corner got to their feet and sidled out. Lord Guy watched them go.

Then he turned his attention to Esther, who was still laughing.

"You are foxed, my sweeting," he said.

Esther stopped laughing. "Is that what it is?" she asked.

"Perhaps. Have some more."

"I would not take any," said Esther, holding out her glass, "were I not persuaded you are mistaken. The warmth from the fire is having a beneficial effect on me."

"We cannot stay here much longer," said Lord Guy. "Two rough-looking men left after they had seen your necklace. They may have gone to find accomplices."

"Fiddle!" laughed Esther, who was feeling wonderfully elated.

"Mayhap they will become lost in the fog, although these rats are used to hunting by night. Darling Esther, I could sit with you here until the end of time, but I fear we might be in danger."

"You have no right to call me Esther," said Esther owlishly. "Not even when we are married. I shall call you Carlton and you shall call me Lady Guy."

"I am glad you have decided to marry me," he said. He took out a piece of paper and held it up. "See! Special license."

"No!" cried Esther. "I was funning. How could you get a special license?"

"One of my second cousins is married to a bishop."

"Why such haste? Why? If and when I get married, the wedding will be set for a year after the engagement, as is proper."

"Dear Esther, under that gloriously prim exterior is a wild and dangerous woman who might marry anyone to spite me. I intend to have you all to myself, and as soon as possible."

"Well, you shan't," said Esther. "This may surprise you, my lord, but I am Untouched!"

"Bravo," he said, amused. "I would not have you any other way."

"Whereas you, my lord, have had many women."

"I have been at the wars a long time," he said. "My . . . er . . . pleasures were few and far between."

"Nonetheless, the idea of any intimacy with such as you repels me."

He put his hands on either side of her face and looked searchingly into her eyes. "You may be right," he said seriously. "I would not have an unwilling bride. Still, it is better to make sure."

He bent his head and kissed her. Esther sat unresponsive in his embrace. Her lips were cold and firm. When he raised his mouth, her eyes were hard.

He looked at her in surprise and dismay.

Then the door of the tap crashed open and four men shouldered their way inside. The landlord, who had been approaching to make up the fire, took one look at them and vaulted back over the counter and disappeared from sight.

Lord Guy rose to his feet, holding his stick as they approached.

It was a silly stick, he reflected vaguely, a small black ebony piece of nonsense with a silver knob and a silver tassel.

Esther rose to her feet as well and stood behind him.

The leader of the four men was squat and burly. "Hand over the gewgaws," he said, "and you won't be hurt."

Lord Guy stood very still, looking at the men. Then, "Stand back," he said to Esther in a low voice.

Esther moved away behind him to the side of the fire, desperately looking about her for a weapon.

Lord Guy continued to stand facing the men. *Why didn't he do something?* thought Esther.

" 'E's struck dumb," said one of the men with a coarse laugh. "Let's get on wiff it, or we'll be 'ere all night."

The leader advanced on Lord Guy.

One minute Lord Guy was standing there, looking at them languidly, the next he moved like lightning. He swung his cane and brought the knob of it down on the leader's head with a sickening crack, and then dodged and feinted as the others rushed in. He threw the next assailant across the tap, swung and kicked the third member of the gang in the teeth, whirled about and seized the punch-bowl and threw the contents in the last man's face. Then he seized Esther by the hand and dragged her out of the tavern, hauling her along the street behind him, until he finally came to a stop.

He pulled her into his arms and held her close while he listened for sounds of pursuit.

All around them the streets hidden in their winding sheets of London fog lay empty and deserted.

"Take me home," whispered Esther, shivering. "I want to go home."

"Then kiss me."

"No."

"I shall keep you here until morning. Kiss me."

"It is not ladylike," said Esther in a choked voice. "Oh, very well."

She could not see his face and her kiss landed on his cheek. He held her tightly and his searching mouth found her own. He buried his lips in hers, ignoring her lack of response, moving his mouth gently on her own, and then more fiercely, until he felt her begin to respond. Esther at first thought she must be drunk. Her legs felt shaky and her arms felt weak. She could not hold out against him. All the punch she had drunk and the fright she had received, combined with the strangeness of the night, took away the last of her defences. If his hands had wandered, if he had tried for further intimacies, she would have taken fright and pushed him away. But for that moment in time, Lord Guy felt that just kissing her was enough. Once he became sure of her response, he settled down to the simple hedonistic delight of kissing someone he loved, adding tenderness to experience, feeling her body come alive, and the heavy weight of her hair beneath his hands as he held the back of her neck.

He did not say anything, fearing that to say words of love, or to demand them, would break the spell. If Miss Esther Jones was content with silent and sometimes savage kissing in the middle of a foggy anonymous London street, then Lord Guy Carlton was happy to give her what she wanted.

The hoarse cry of the watch sounding from far away brought them back to reality.

"I would never be sure," said Esther in a low, shaky voice, "that you were faithful to me."

"Every man does silly things at some time in his life," he said. "If only you had done something silly, Esther, then you would be glad of the shelter of my unrespectable arms. Take a risk. Marry me. Surely even the respectable Miss Jones knows she cannot kiss a man in a London street and *not* marry him. I could gossip, you know, and damn you as a wanton."

"But you will not."

"Ah, if I am such a paragon, then I am respectable enough for you. By all that's holy, I hear a carriage."

The sound of horses' hooves plodding along came to their ears.

"Hey!" called Lord Guy. "I say, driver!"

The bulk of a carriage loomed up, a blacker blackness in the fog.

"I'm lost," came a plaintive voice from the box. "Strothers is the name. You sound like a gentleman."

"George Strothers!" cried Lord Guy. "It is I, Carlton."

Lord Guy turned to Esther. "One of my drinking companions," he said. He turned back to the carriage. "Strothers, take us up and get us somewhere civilised."

"Can't," said Mr. Strothers. "Try your hand with the ribbons if you like, Carlton, but I've been driving my poor beasts around and around for hours trying to find the way home."

Mr. Strothers slid along to the passenger seat, and Lord Guy helped Esther up onto the box. Lord Guy took the reins, and, with Esther between them, they set out through the fog.

By dint of stopping when they saw a linkboy's torch and by diligently asking every shape they could see in the fog, Lord Guy and Esther managed to pilot the carriage up into Broad Street, along Broad Street to High Street and then into Oxford Street, down Bond Street, round into Hay Hill and so into Berkeley Square. Esther and Lord Guy thanked Mr. Strothers and sent him on his way to his house in Hill Street off Berkeley Square. Esther thought it odd that she did not even know what Mr. Strothers looked like.

To her distress, Lord Guy followed her into her home. She was overset with the events of the evening, the effects of the punch were melting away, and she was becoming horrified at her own behaviour. Miss Fipps appeared in her undress, wearing quite the largest nightcap Lord Guy could ever remember seeing. She cooed with distress over Esther's adventures, her faded eyes wide with distress, and Esther, who had planned to dismiss Miss Fipps, found herself glad of her companion's motherly concern.

But no sooner had Miss Fipps seen the couple furnished with the tea-tray and warmed by a roaring fire than she smiled gently on both of them and drifted out of the room, leaving them alone together.

"A fine chaperone I have chosen," said Esther bitterly.

"As far as my cousin is concerned," said Lord Guy, "we are engaged and *want* to be together. Come! Drink your tea and go to bed. I have no intention of laying a finger on you. This repellent room is enough to put anyone off."

"This is a charming and well-furnished room," said Esther hotly.

He raised one eyebrow and looked from the open Bible to the grim furniture and the gloomy hangings.

"You see!" went on Esther when he did not reply. "Why should I marry? Why should I have my taste criticised and the equilibrium of my life upset?"

"For love," he said, putting down his teacup. He rose to his feet and she shrank back in her chair. "I am not going to kiss you," he said. "Good night, Miss Jones."

His face was suddenly older, tired and drawn, and his blue eyes were serious. He bowed and left.

Esther sat alone, looking at the fire. Perhaps he had taken her in dislike and would go away and never see her again. Her head began to ache, and she reflected that punch had a very lowering effect on the spirits.

Lord Guy let himself in at 67 Clarges Street. Three of his servants were waiting for him in the hall, Rainbird, Angus MacGregor, and Joseph.

"There was no need for you all to wait up for me," said Lord Guy, somewhat touched.

But the idea that they had been waiting up to see to his needs was soon banished as Rainbird said, "We have a most important matter to discuss with you, my lord."

"Come into the front parlour," he said with a sigh. "Mr. Roger at home?"

"He has not come back from White's."

"Oh, is that where's he's gone? Then he won't be back until morning. Out with it, Rainbird. What is it?"

Rainbird produced a small black notebook. "We have reason to believe your servant, Manuel, is a French spy," he said. "We took the liberty of searching his clothes when he was asleep. We found this. It is all in Spanish and none of us can read Spanish."

"I've never heard such nonsense," said Lord Guy wearily. "Pass it over."

There were only two pages of writing. He read them carefully and then a smile curled his lips. "Do you want me to read this to you?" he asked.

"If you please, my lord," said Rainbird.

"Very well. It begins, 'I do not like this household. The butler is a mountebank who does not behave like a butler at all. He is quite ill-favoured and smells bad. The chef is a barbarian, a Scotchman who speaks a savage language. He has a foul temper. The footman is a . . .'" Lord Guy raised his eyebrows. "I really don't think I ought to go on," he said. "I suggest you replace this and do not interfere with my servant's personal property again. It appears that people who read other people's notebooks are like people who listen at keyholes. They never hear any good of themselves."

Rainbird took the book, and the three servants shuffled out.

"The wee sneak," fumed Angus, "writing all thae nasty things."

"I wonder what he wrote about me?" asked Joseph. "We stayed awake for nothing and I'm that tired. Me and Lizzie walked and walked and thought we'd never get home."

Manuel opened one eye as they slid the book back into his pocket. Then he closed it again and smiled to himself as he went back to sleep.

Chapter Nine

When Charlotte first increased the Cyprian corps,
She asked a hundred pounds—I gave her more.
Next year to fifty sunk the course of trade,
I thought it now extravagant, but paid.
Six months elaps'd, 'twas twenty guineas then;
In vain I prayed, and press'd and profferr'd ten.
Another quarter barely flip'd away,
She begged FOUR GUINEAS of me at the play:
I haggled—her demand still humbler grew,
'Twas "thank you kindly, sir" for two pounds two.
Next, in the street her favours I might win
For a few shillings and a glass of gin.
—And now (though sad and wonderful it sounds)
I would not touch her for a hundred pounds.

—ANON

The sickening, choking fog clung on all the next day. There seemed no chance of Esther going to society, but, to her surprise, society came to her.

Finally drawn as if by a magnet by the lure of her great wealth, carriages rolled up and men and women of the ton descended in droves.

Amy and Peter were delighted, for an Esther coping with a saloonful of the beau monde had no time to attend to their lessons. Furthermore, she did not know it was not fashionable to have children present, and Peter and Amy were made much of by the members of the ton, who judged that the road to Miss Jones' heart was through the hearts of her little brother and sister.

At first, Esther felt at a loss. She did not have any conversation, or rather, any that was acceptable. Her interest in the wars with Napoleon, the welfare of servants, and the current political climate were items of too base a coin to offer guests who rattled on at an amazing rate about a great deal of people she did not know. There was much talk also of the Prince of Wales' penchant for elderly ladies, some claiming that his taste in mistresses showed a desire for common and sentimental domesticity rather than nights of erotic passion.

And then Lord Guy was ushered in. He smoothly took over the role of host in such an expert way that several adventurers who had still had hopes of catching the eye of the heiress shortly took their leave. Esther was able to relax and attend to the simple duties of seeing everyone had enough to eat and drink while Lord Guy chatted lightly of this and that. How a man who had only been a short time in Town could amass such an amazing amount of trivial society gossip was startling to Esther. She would have liked to despise him, but her better nature told her that he was saving her from a great deal of embarrassment and, at the same time, giving her a social gloss.

He stayed for fifteen minutes and then offered to take the children out with their pony, Snowball, and their new cart to see how Peter handled the ribbons.

With glowing faces, Peter and Amy went off with him, one child hanging on to each hand.

Esther, who had spent the morning drafting out an

advertisement announcing the termination of her engagement, began to realise that, despite her money, without Lord Guy she would find it very hard to be on terms with any of these people. She wondered whether she had basically a very common soul, since she would actually have preferred to have a comfortable cose with Rainbird. He had called briefly in the morning, and she had taxed him with the case of Miss Fipps.

But Rainbird had pointed out that Miss Fipps, although she happened to be Lord Guy's cousin, was an estimable lady and there were very few of those around. He added that if Miss Fipps had initially announced she was Lord Guy's cousin, then Miss Jones would not have hired her, and both ladies would have therefore lost the chance of suitable companionship.

Soothed as ever by Rainbird's common sense, Esther had offered him a post in her household. He had said he would need a little time to consider the matter, but Esther was sure he meant to refuse.

That a mere servant should put loyalty to his friends above money was a new idea to her. Hitherto, Esther had never considered any of the lower orders as individuals. She saw them as a sort of anonymous mass. Rainbird had opened her eyes to that other world.

It was an awakening that was to be Esther's social undoing.

As the uneasiness of war and the threat of invasion once more gripped London, society paradoxically seemed more hell-bent on frivolity than ever. The Dandies, led by their king, Mr. George Brummell, sat in the clubs of St. James' polishing their wit—usually quite horrendous puns. A roomful of Dandies could talk for hours about their clothes without a glint of humour.

The laws of society became more rigid as London was

engulfed in the greatest wave of snobbery ever known. Sons openly cut their mothers if they considered their appearance to be at all at fault, daughters tried to commit suicide if their vouchers to the famous Almack's Assembly Rooms were not forthcoming.

Perhaps Lord Guy's flippant remark about his servants' being like a tribe should have been applied to his peers. Esther was entering a world of peculiar shibboleths and taboos, and she had as much knowledge of them as an Elizabethan explorer encountering American Indians for the first time.

Because of her father's scandalous country life, Esther had kept herself isolated from her peers, and so Miss Fipps did not know the extent of her employer's social ignorance. Although Esther could not be accounted in the first bloom of youth—Miss Fipps was used to ladies' absorbing the dos and don'ts of social behaviour by a sort of osmosis.

That Esther wished to appear at the opera for the very start of the performance was a harmless eccentricity in Miss Fipps' eyes.

So when the dreadful fog blew away and sunny skies shone over sooty London and the air was once more warm with spring, the two ladies set out for the opera, both comfortably feeling fashionable and elegant and secure.

Esther was wearing a gown of French net over white satin, painted in "natural" flowers. On her head, she wore a new tiara of amethysts, having learned from Miss Fipps that diamonds were "quite exploded, my dear." She had had her hair cut so that her burnished red curls covered her head like a cap. She wondered if Lord Guy would be angry because she had had her hair shorn, and then told herself angrily it did not matter what he thought.

Miss Fipps wore a round train dress of Moravian muslin, fastened up the sides with clasps of gold. To her relief,

Esther had chastised her only mildly for having kept the secret of her relationship with Lord Guy. Miss Fipps was even more devoted to Esther than ever, but nonetheless she had sent a note to Lord Guy to inform him they would be attending the opera.

Esther was disappointed in the production, which was called *The Harlequin's Revenge* and had been written by a Mr. Dyer "in the Italian manner." It was a silly piece of nonsense, and Esther's attention strayed to the audience.

"There are a great number of ladies in the centre boxes without escorts," she whispered to Miss Fipps.

"Prostitutes," said Miss Fipps. "Do not look. Oh, there is Mr. Brummell and Lord Alvanley, and see, just entering, there is Lord Petersham. He has a different kind of snuff for every day of the year."

But Esther found her eyes being drawn back to the prostitutes. Had Miss Fipps not told her what they were, she would have taken them for ladies of fashion. In an age when women wore less than they had ever done but wore just as much blanc and rouge, there was little difference between the ladies in the side boxes and the ladies in the centre.

And then she saw a little drama being played out in one of the centre boxes. She raised her opera glasses. What was going on was more intriguing than the performance on the stage.

A young girl, finely dressed in white muslin, sat in tears in one of the centre boxes. She looked about sixteen years of age. She had thick fair hair and a flawless complexion that owed nothing to paint. She had large brown eyes and a neat figure. Her bosom was generous, and her gown had been cut low to display its charms. She kept putting an arm across her breasts, and the elderly hard-faced woman who sat with her kept roughly pushing her arm down and scolding her. Tears ran down the girl's cheeks without making her eyes red.

Esther nudged Miss Fipps. "That little beauty," she said, nodding her head in the direction of the centre box, "cannot be a prostitute. She looks much too innocent."

Miss Fipps cast a worldly eye in the same direction and sighed. "She is, at the moment. Fresh come from the country, I should imagine."

"Is she that awful-looking woman's daughter, think you?"

"No, no," said Miss Fipps, "she is an abbess." And, seeing the puzzled frown of Esther's face, explained, "The owner of a brothel. You see, they wait around the agencies looking for servant girls fresh up from the country. They hire the girl and set the bully-boys on her. She is not seduced, that would reduce her price. She is taken here and put on display. Before the evening is out, some gentleman will offer a high price for her."

"But it should be stopped!" said Esther, appalled. "The law . . ."

"There is no law for such as she," said Miss Fipps.

Esther sat biting her lip in distress and Miss Fipps began to feel anxious. She wished Lord Guy would put in an appearance. It was most odd of Esther to anguish over the fate of an about-to-be prostitute. There were prostitutes everywhere; one could hardly move without tripping over one. But a lady never noticed them.

Because London was still policed much as it had been in Shakespeare's time, east of St. James' was an inferno of crime. The policing of London was completely ineffectual, an antiquated hotchpotch of parish officers, beadles, constables, watchmen, and street keepers. It was hopelessly out of date in its traditional organisation, belonging to a cluster of parishes and not to a city whose population was nearly a million. The strongest permanent force, which was that of the City of London itself, had only about forty-five men, directed by two City marshals. The famous Bow Street had only a few more men, chiefly for patrol duties, than the other London magistrates courts, which had at their disposal only eight to twelve policemen. The forces of law and order stopped very short outside the boundaries of society and were hard to find in the hundreds of alleys and narrow, badly lighted streets that made up the most of London.

The girl in the centre box was crying harder than ever. Esther felt her own eyes begin to water with sympathetic tears.

"And does she sit there like a cow at auction waiting for some gentleman to call at the box and buy?" she asked.

"I think she will be taken to Fops Alley at the second interval and be put on display," said Miss Fipps.

To her relief, Esther appeared to lose interest in the girl. But still Miss Fipps worried over the non-appearance of her cousin.

Joseph was in deep disgrace. This time, if he had been attacked by Manuel with a long stiletto, no one would have been in the least surprised.

The laundering of Lord Guy's fine linen was done in the kitchen, Mrs. Middleton being proud of the work of Jenny and Alice. Sheets and huckaback towels were sent out to the washerwoman when there was a great number to be laundered, but shirts and cravats were washed, ironed, and starched at Number 67.

Joseph had trodden on a rusty nail, which had stabbed through the thin sole of his shoe. He was afraid of infection and had asked Angus to boil him a pan of water. Alice had put a large copper pan of water on to boil, in which she

meant to wash Lord Guy's cravats. She then had gone upstairs to change the bed linen, and while she was away,
Joseph, thinking the water was for his foot and not seeing
the cravats in it, had added a generous helping of potassi-
um-permanganate crystals.

When he lifted the pan down to bathe his foot, he saw
the cravats.

It was then Manuel had come into the kitchen demanding a clean cravat for my lord. And that was when they
discovered that the Spanish servant had given them *all*
Lord Guy's cravats, along with all those belonging to Mr.
Roger, and that all the cravats were now bright pink. The
servants were sent running throughout London to try to
purchase new cravats while Lord Guy fretted over the
delay. He did not know whether to be angrier with Manuel
or with Joseph, because, for some strange reason, the Spanish servant had sent at least six clean cravats down to the
kitchen to be washed along with the dirty ones.

It was Angus MacGregor who finally tore a shopkeeper
away from his family supper and managed to purchase new
ones.

Lord Guy set out for the opera with Mr. Roger, who
tried to comfort him by pointing out that they would be
there before the end, at least by the second interval.

Esther received many callers in her box during the first
interval, most of whom had just arrived. One was Lady
Jersey, a patroness of Almack's. Mrs. Fipps was in high alt.
"There will be no trouble with your vouchers now," she
whispered after Lady Jersey had left.

Miss Fipps was glad to notice that although Esther
appeared to be lost in thought during the next act of the
opera, her eyes no longer strayed to the centre boxes.

And so no frisson of approaching social doom troubled Miss Fipps when, at the beginning of the second interval, Esther murmured she was stepping outside for a few moments.

It was only when Lord Guy and Mr. Roger arrived, demanding Esther's whereabouts, that Miss Fipps began to become worried.

"Miss Jones said she was just stepping outside for a moment," she said.

"May as well wait," said Mr. Roger. "Probably gone to call on a friend."

"Hasn't got any," said Lord Guy laconically, raising his glass and studying the house.

"My dear Carlton," said Miss Fipps, much shocked. "She has me!"

Lord Guy noticed that various gentlemen returning to their boxes after a stroll in Fops Alley appeared to be in a high state of excitement. They bent their heads and whispered to their female companions, and then all eyes focussed avidly on Esther's box.

"Why is it," said Lord Guy, lowering his glass, "that I have the uneasy feeling my beloved has just managed to disgrace herself in some quite shocking way?"

"Oh dear," said Miss Fipps with a start. "She *wouldn't.*"

"Wouldn't what?" asked Mr. Roger.

"For a moment she became upset because one of the ladies of cracked reputation in the centre boxes was putting an innocent up for sale. She asked me if the gentlemen would call at her box to put in their bids, and I said she would probably be promenaded in Fops Alley at the second interval. But Miss Jones would never . . ."

"Yes, she would," said Lord Guy. "The deuce!"

He rose to his feet, but at that very moment the door at the back of the box opened and Esther entered, pushing the little country girl in front of her.

"I have hired a new maid," she said haughtily. "This is Charlotte. Pray take a seat behind me, Charlotte." The girl meekly did as she was bid. Miss Fipps fanned herself vigorously and looked to Lord Guy for help.

"Am I right, Miss Jones," said Lord Guy, "in assuming you had the temerity to rescue that fair blossom from Fops Alley?"

"Yes," said Esther, "and a most embarrassing time I had of it. You would never believe people could be so unfeeling. I appealed to some of the gentlemen for help, and they treated me . . . most rudely. I was obliged to slap two of them and kick a third. Fortunately, I always carry a great deal of money with me. It cost me one hundred guineas for that poor girl. Can you imagine? Just a little more than I paid for that mare. That horrible woman who was trying to corrupt her had the gall to ask for double. I told her I would take her to court."

Mr. Roger looked wonderingly round at the boxes near him, which were full of shocked and disapproving faces. "Were you interested in making your début in society, Miss Jones?" he asked.

"Yes," said Esther. "I have Come Out."

"I really think, ma'am, you're back *in*," said Mr. Roger. "They'll never forgive you."

"What! For rescuing that poor child!"

"A lady," said Lord Guy, "is not supposed to be aware of the existence of prostitutes. I think it politic to take our leave now."

"No," said Esther firmly. "I have done my duty. I intend to stay until the end and go to the ball and supper afterwards."

"As you please," said Lord Guy. "But I doubt if they'll let you in. Do you intend to take your new maid to the ball with you?"

"Of course."

Lord Guy swivelled round and studied Charlotte. She was gazing at Esther with adoring eyes.

"Talk sense to her, Carlton," cried Miss Fipps, but he shook his head and murmured, "Be quiet. This might serve very well."

Esther grimly faced the stage and appeared to pay intent interest to the rest of the opera. She fought down a nagging fear she had indeed disgraced herself. But it could not be true! She had behaved well. No one with any heart or feelings could see such as Charlotte in distress.

The opera finally dragged to an end.

Esther rose to leave.

"Wait but a little, Miss Jones," pleaded Miss Fipps. "Wait until those rough gentlemen you spoke of have made their exit."

"Very well," said Esther reluctantly. "Perhaps you could lend Charlotte your stole, Miss Fipps. The scantiness of her gown is causing her acute embarrassment."

Miss Fipps handed her silk stole to Charlotte, who shyly murmured thanks and wrapped it tightly about the low neckline of her gown. The girl was amazingly contented now, thought Lord Guy. Her trust in Esther appeared to be absolute.

Mr. Roger opened his mouth to protest, to make a last stand against the humiliation he was sure awaited Esther, but before he could get the words out, Lord Guy stamped on his foot, and he gave a yelp of pain instead.

Esther, head held high, walked out of the box on Lord Guy's arm. Mr. Roger offered one arm to Miss Fipps, and, after some hesitation, the other to Charlotte.

As they approached the open double doors leading to the ballroom, Lord Guy grimly noticed all eyes were turned to those doors, waiting.

Esther made to enter the ballroom. A liveried official placed his long gold-topped staff across the door, barring the way.

"What is the meaning of this?" demanded Esther haughtily.

On the other side of the barrier created by the staff appeared two members of the opera committee, Lord Fremand and the Countess of Weighton.

"You have disgraced yourself, Miss Jones," said the countess. "You must leave."

"I was helping a child in distress."

"You created a vulgar brawl over a prostitute," said the countess icily. "Is that not so, Fremand?"

But the elderly Lord Fremand bowed his head and did not reply. He was afraid Lord Guy might call him out.

"You disgust me! All of you!" cried Esther, her eyes flashing. "You can keep your ball and your opera box and your shoddy moral standards. *You* are the disgrace, not I. Come, Lord Guy."

"Yes, ma'am," he said meekly.

Two Fops were standing at the top of the grand staircase. As Esther passed, one of them jeered, "So that's how you make your money, you abbess. Let us know when you've set a price on the little beauty there."

Lord Guy smiled pleasantly before he drove his fist into one of the Fops' noses. Mr. Roger, with a growl like a bear, proceeded to demolish the other.

Esther's lip began to tremble. *Amy and Peter,* she thought wildly. *I have ruined their futures.*

She walked on down the stairs. Miss Fipps was sobbing into her handkerchief. Esther felt dreadful.

A final crash and yell from behind her rounded off the end of the fight. Lord Guy and Mr. Roger caught up with her.

Outside the theatre, Esther turned to Lord Guy and held out her hand. "Thank you for your championship, my lord," she said. "I do not expect to see you again."

Before Lord Guy could reply, a watchman came creaking up. "Careful how you go," he said. "The mob's out."

"What is it this time?" asked Mr. Roger.

"Sir Francis Burdett," said the watchman, and proceeded to explain. Sir Francis, a popular reformer, had put forward the theory that the House of Commons had no right to imprison people. It appeared the House had just proved him wrong by shutting him up in the Tower of London. The London mob was on the rampage and crying for blood.

Lord Guy thought quickly. "We had better all go in my carriage," he said to Esther. "We may not get very far."

Esther was by now too demoralised to make any protest. Manuel and an ostler brought Lord Guy's carriage around. He sent Manuel off on foot to Clarges Street, telling him to make sure the shutters were up on all the windows.

After retrieving a brace of horse pistols, he ushered the ladies inside and climbed up on the box, with Mr. Roger beside him.

He handed a pistol to Mr. Roger and took one himself.

"Why didn't you stop her!" marvelled Mr. Roger.

"Because, Tommy, she is more likely to fall off her pedestal into my arms. I know how to restore her reputation, but before that, I want her as my wife."

"Hope I never get one of these grand passions," said Mr. Roger. "Too exhausting."

"Never mind," said Lord Guy with a grin. "It has its compensations. Hold tight, Tommy. I'll keep to the back streets."

At first they thought they were going to be lucky and

that the mob might be confining its activities around Westminster, or over at the Tower, but as they drove into Berkeley Square, they were surrounded on all sides by a roaring and dangerous crowd.

"I'll fire over their heads," shouted Mr. Roger.

"No," said Lord Guy. "I have a better idea."

He stopped the coach and stood up on the box. He raised his arms and cried, "Make way, my friends, I have a cholera victim."

Cholera. That dreadful word spread out throughout the mob. The ringleaders backed away from the coach, stumbling over the people behind them in their haste to escape.

"They'll come to their senses shortly and realise that grandly dressed ladies returning from the opera are not cholera victims," said Lord Guy. "But we may be able to get Esther home safely."

Outside Esther's home, he called to the ladies to get out quickly. "Go into the house with them and stay there," he said to Mr. Roger. "I will try to return as soon as possible."

"Where are you going?"

"I am going to the mews. I am not leaving these good animals to be mauled and terrified and tortured by the mob."

"Hurry, then," cried Mr. Roger, jumping down. "I think I hear them coming back."

Chapter
Ten

Confess, ye volunteers,
Lieutenant and Ensign,
And Captain of the line,
As bold as Roman—
Confess, ye grenadiers,
However strong and tall,
The Conqueror of you all
Is Woman, Woman!

—THACKERAY

Esther had much to keep her occupied for the first hour. Her housekeeper, Mrs. Troubridge, was told that Charlotte had just arrived unexpectedly from the country. She was to be given a room in the servants' quarters, supplied with a print gown, and was to enter into her duties on the following day. No mention was made of Charlotte's near recruitment into the Cyprians.

Then Mr. Roger was pressed to stay the night. Although a room was prepared for him, he elected to stay awake and armed in case the mob should try to break in.

Amy and Peter were almost too excited to go to sleep.

They had watched the arrival from the nursery window and Lord Guy was even more of a hero in their eyes. Esther did not have the heart to tell them of her great disgrace—a disgrace that would surely terminate her engagement to Lord Guy. The tables had turned with a vengeance. Now it was Miss Esther Jones who was not fit to be the bride of Lord Guy Carlton.

She changed out of her opera gown into a blue muslin gown and then went downstairs to the gloomy saloon to wait and wonder if Lord Guy had escaped unscathed from the mob, and if he would return that evening.

Mr. Roger, sitting by the fire with his pistol on his lap, made desultory conversation. After a while his eyelids began to droop and his head to nod.

A thundering knocking at the outside door made him jerk awake.

"No," he said as Esther rose to her feet, "I'd better answer it."

He went into the hall and pushed aside the butler, Graves, who was grey with fright.

"Who is there?" called Mr. Roger.

"It is I, Carlton," came Lord Guy's voice.

Mr. Roger unlocked and unbolted the door. Lord Guy strode in. He had changed out of his evening dress into riding dress—buff coat, leather breeches, and top-boots.

"I say, Tommy," he said, "has Miss Jones gone to bed yet?"

"No, she is in the saloon."

"I think it would be wise if you made your way to Clarges Street while there is a temporary lull in the rioting. Someone needs to be there to help them guard the place. Try, if you can, to find out why Manuel tried to stop me going to the opera. I cannot think he got rid of all my cravats out of sheer stupidity. Where is Miss Fipps?"

"She has retired. The evening was a bit of strain. She feels she has let Miss Jones down by not preventing her from making a fool of herself."

"I do not think Miss Jones made a fool of herself at all. We can turn the tables when the rioting dies down. In the meantime, leave the field to me, if you take my meaning, and be prepared to act as bride's man at a moment's notice."

Mr. Roger winked and let himself out into the night.

Lord Guy turned to the hovering butler. "I feel sure we shall not need your services this night, Graves," he said. "But sleep in your clothes and ask the other manservants to do the same in case we are attacked."

"Very good, my lord," said Graves.

Lord Guy strode into the saloon and stood looking at Esther.

"Oh, my love," he said. "What have you done to your hair?"

"How like you, my lord," said Esther with a faint smile. "The whole of London is in peril and yet all you can notice is a lady's hair."

"The most important thing in the world," he said softly. "Well, my sweeting, that was the briefest and most dramatic coming-out I am ever likely to witness."

"Do not mock me," said Esther. "At least I can now release you from our engagement with an easy conscience."

"No, that you cannot," he said severely. "Only think of poor Amy and Peter."

"They are young and will soon forget."

"But society will never forget," said Lord Guy, mentally sending up a prayer for forgiveness, as he was sure the terror of the mob would have already driven Esther's scandal from the minds of the ton. The fear of a revolution taking place in Britain, like the one that had rocked France, was never far from their minds. "You had better marry me," he said. "We will go abroad, and when we return, everything will be forgotten."

"I thought you said society would *never* forget," said Esther sharply.

"Did I? I meant for some time. Faith, the night is chilly and you so charmingly attired in thin muslin."

He walked over to the fireplace, and, crouching down in front of it, began to pile it high with logs and coal. Then he sat back on his heels and looked at her, noticing for the first time the strain in her eyes.

They were oddly beautiful eyes, he thought. Because of her dress, they looked blue. They seemed to pick up the colour of whatever she was wearing. He was very near her as she sat by the fire, and his face was almost on a level with her own.

From outside in the square came a muffled roar and the sound of shots. Esther shivered.

He leaned forward and gently drew her face to his own.

"No," whispered Esther.

He stroked her face with his long fingers. "If you loved me," he said quietly, "then that lot out there could burn London and you would not care. There is another kind of scorching and burning, my sweet Esther. Come, let me teach you."

"I would learn none of your wanton tricks," said Esther in a voice that trembled.

"And I would teach you none," he said huskily. "I would teach you to love me." Kneeling in front of her, he held her by the shoulders and kissed her lips. She made a murmur of protest. A shot rattled just then against the shutters, and with an alarmed cry, she fell forward into his arms.

He drew her down onto the hearthrug and pressed his lips to hers. Esther felt her senses beginning to swim. She looked up dizzily over his shoulder, and the stern face of the reformer over the fireplace stared back.

Another shot struck the shutters. "The children!" cried Esther, pulling away.

"They will do very well," he said. "Children can sleep through anything. Oh, kiss me again, my stern Miss Jones. Your mouth is sweet, and I would lose myself in it."

Esther moaned a protest as his clever hands and experienced mouth took control of her senses. He kissed and kissed until Esther went down before wave after wave of passion. He seemed to be wearing a great deal of clothes compared to her own flimsy covering, which was no protection from roving hands and searching, questing mouth. He shifted her body a little away from the fire as the flames blazed higher. He sat up and removed his cravat and jacket and then tossed his waistcoat in the corner.

"No, you must not . . . you cannot," said Esther, trying to fight against the drugged feeling in her body.

He laughed down at her dazed eyes as he stripped off his shirt.

"Murder them! Burn them!" screamed a voice outside.

"Stop!" whispered Esther. "Please stop."

But his hands had found the tapes that held her dress. The material whispered down her shoulders to bare her breasts. She put up her arms to try to cover them, but he smiled at her gently, and said, "I will hide them for you."

He jerked her back into his arms and pressed her naked breasts against his bare chest.

The effect on Esther's senses was devastating. Something seemed to give inside her, and she began to kiss him back with ferocity and passion.

A volley of shots sounded in the square outside as the militia moved in to quell the mob. There were screams and howls, but Miss Esther Jones lay in Lord Guy Carlton's arms deaf and blind to the outside world. For Lord Guy, no horrible scenes of battle disturbed his mind. She was moaning in abject surrender as he kissed one perfect breast when all at once his lovemaking ceased. He gave her a little shake.

"Don't stop," pleaded Esther.

"Marry me tomorrow."

"Oh, Carlton . . ."

"My name is Guy. Marry me tomorrow. I will have all of you in the wedding bed and nowhere else. Marry me!"

"Yes," said Esther. "Oh, yes."

"We will be married here, a quiet wedding, and when London returns to normal, we will be married in church."

"You, in church?" said Esther. "Do you not know, my lord, it is deemed monstrous unfashionable to be married in church?"

"I'll have you, Esther Jones, before man *and* God. Now, kiss me again and send me on my way. I shall return tomorrow with the preacher. I dare not stay here because I would not be able to keep my hands off you."

The sounds in the square outside were dying away. He dressed, gave Esther a hard kiss on the lips, and took his leave.

Ten minutes later, Lord Guy roused the staff and Mr. Roger at Number 67 Clarges Street to tell them of his forthcoming wedding. They all cheered. Rainbird ran down the stairs to fetch champagne. Only Manuel stood grim and silent. He could see all his hopes and dreams fading away. After the celebrations were over, after he had heard Mr. Roger teasing Lord Guy over breaking the conventions by staying alone with his bride-to-be before the wedding night, and staff and masters had at last gone happily to bed, Manuel stayed behind in the front parlour beside the dying fire and made his plans.

Graves, hollow-cheeked and white of face, opened the

door to Manuel the following morning and wearily heard the Spanish servant say he had an urgent message for Miss Jones from Lord Guy Carlton. In vain did Mr. Graves protest it was too early in the day; Manuel was adamant. Miss Jones would be most incensed if she did not receive my lord's message.

When Esther finally came downstairs in her undress, Manuel, eyeing Graves, said he preferred to speak to her in private.

"Very well," said Esther, surveying the servant with dislike. Could she persuade Guy to get rid of him once they were married?

At first she could not quite take in what Manuel was trying to tell her. She shook her head in confusion and asked him, "I am sorry. I am so tired. What are you saying?"

"I am saying that my lord is leaving for Portugal today," said Manuel.

"But we are to be married today!"

Manuel shook his head sadly. "A great joke of it he made last night, did my lord. 'She thinks I am to wed her,' he say, and he laugh, and all the servants laugh and drink champagne. My lord, he say he give anything to see your face when you find him gone."

"I do not believe you," said Esther, white-lipped.

"Madam, this is a painful and disgusting task for me. If I lie, I lose my employ and find myself alone in this foreign country. Why should I lie?"

"Please leave me," said Esther. "I must think."

"Go, madam," said Manuel. "Do not stay in London to let the ton know your humiliation. Go! Go, quickly!"

"Leave me!" cried Esther.

Manuel slid out, but he went only as far as the opposite side of the square, where he waited, watching the house.

He was a desperate man, and that desperation had made him stupid. Had Esther been a normal society lady, she would have promptly called at her fiancé's home and demanded an explanation. But he did not know how lucky he was. For Esther, deep in humiliation, could only remember with hot cheeks the liberties she had allowed Lord Guy. She remembered the scandal her father had caused when he had promised marriage to a miss in the neighbouring county who did not know until she had been shamed and ridiculed that the squire was already married. *Rakes were all the same,* thought Esther bitterly. But he should not find out that she had spent the day waiting like a fool for the preacher.

Brighton. That was it. She would go to Brighton and take the children with her. There was Miss Fipps, and Miss Fipps was Lord Guy's cousin. But she had already proved herself an affectionate friend. Esther would tell Miss Fipps about it all when they arrived in Brighton. If she told her before then, she felt sure Miss Fipps would rush to Clarges Street to give Lord Guy a piece of her mind and the wretched philanderer would know how badly she, Esther, had been hurt. Thank goodness she had not told the children, Miss Fipps, or the household about the wedding.

After two hours, Manuel's waiting was rewarded. A cumbersome travelling carriage pulled up outside Esther's home. After a little while, Esther appeared, heavily veiled, leading the children and followed by Miss Fipps and her lady's maid. Trunks were strapped up behind.

In the distance, Manuel heard the baying of the mob, who had risen afresh and were hell-bent on destroying everything in sight. He took to his heels and ran.

Lord Guy Carlton decided to see Esther again before going off to find the vicar. The vicar, the Reverend Abraham Pascombe, was an old friend, albeit a drunken and disgraceful one. But Lord Guy felt he would serve the purpose and perform adequately.

Lord Guy walked round to Berkeley Square with a brace of pistols in his pocket. He had to pick his way through shards of glass and broken shutters. Somewhere nearby, the mob had started to burn houses, and the air was heavy with the smell of smoke. London waited for another onslaught from the rabble. The cannon in St. James' Park had been loaded with ball. A party of Burdettites from Soho rounded the corner with blue cockades and colours flying. They did not try to stop him, contenting themselves with shouting, "Burdett forever. Magna Carta. Trial by jury." Most of them seemed to be in an advanced state of intoxication.

Lord Guy almost welcomed their presence. It proved that, with or without Esther, he was cured of his nightmares of the battlefield. One of their number fired a gun in the air, and Lord Guy did not even flinch.

He knocked at Esther's door and waited some time before a cautious voice on the inside could be heard demanding his name and business.

Then he had to wait until the bolts were slid back and the door unlocked.

"Miss Jones?" he said, striding past Graves into the hall.

"Madam has left," said Graves.

"When? Why? Where?"

"An hour ago. I do not know. Miss Jones has gone to Brighton," said Graves, answering each question in turn.

"Good Gad. Did she leave no message, no letter?"

"No, my lord."

If Esther had appeared in front of him at that moment, he felt he would cheerfully have strangled her. No man of his rank and breeding could tolerate such an insult from a woman.

His face hard and set, he turned to leave.

But Graves, who was still annoyed with the way the pampered servants of Clarges Street appeared to demand audience with his mistress anytime they felt like it, said sourly to his retreating back, "Miss Jones decided to leave immediately after receiving a message from your lordship's servant. I assumed that because of the dangers in Town, your lordship had suggested Miss Jones remove herself and the children to Brighton."

"Manuel!" said Lord Guy between his teeth.

He turned and strode out of the door, leaving Graves looking after him.

At Clarges Street, he roused Mr. Roger from his bed and told him of the happenings of the morning. "Told you the fellow was up to no good," said Mr. Roger. "What are you going to do?"

"Come down to the parlour with me and let's have him in, unless he has run away."

Mr. Roger swathed his burly form in a Chinese dressing-gown and followed Lord Guy downstairs. Lord Guy rang the bell and when Rainbird appeared he curtly ordered Manuel to be brought in.

Manuel had not fled. He was confident his plan had worked. He was sitting in his attic room busily writing when Rainbird told him he was wanted.

"I come soon," he said, picking up his papers and stuffing them in his pocket.

"You'd better come sharpish," said Rainbird. "My lord looks like death."

Rainbird stood by the door of the front parlour until Manuel came downstairs. He held open the door, ushered Manuel in, and closed it behind him.

"What did you tell my fiancée?" demanded Lord Guy harshly.

"I did not tell her anything, my lord. I think you go there and go myself to attend to your wishes."

"You could have looked in my bedroom. I am curious about you, Manuel. Very curious." Lord Guy drew a pistol out of his pocket and levelled it at him. "If you make a move, I will blow your head off. Tommy, search him."

Manuel made a dive for the door. Lord Guy fired a ball over his head into the woodwork, and Manuel stood stock-still, white-faced and trembling.

"Now, Tommy," said Lord Guy grimly.

Tommy seized Manuel by the scruff of his neck with one large hand and ferreted in his pockets with the other. He drew out a black notebook and a sheaf of papers and newspaper cuttings. He kept hold of the servant while he tossed them over to Lord Guy.

He studied them in amazement. The notebook contained details of everything that had happened since Manuel had taken up the post as his servant. There were also cuttings from an American newspaper called the *Sun*.

Rainbird, Angus, and Joseph came bursting into the room, having heard the shot. They stood looking amazed at the smoking gun in Lord Guy's hand and the wretched Manuel being held in Mr. Roger's hands.

"If you are a spy," said Lord Guy heavily, "you are a damned inept one. There is not one thing here that is not common knowledge. Who are you? Speak before I shoot you."

Manuel fell to his knees. "Don't shoot," he pleaded. "I only want to be a great journalist, like Monsieur Cavet. Like him, I am a Frenchman."

"I thought your country was Spain."

"I am French by birth. I was born in Agde. My father,

he is Spanish. My mother was French. My father married again, an Englishwoman, who taught me her language. I knew I would have to be cautious when we reached Spain, for I speak Spanish with a French accent. I wish to be a journalist for the American papers like Monsieur Cavet. But the newspaper told me they did not want the reports of London society, they wanted my experiences at war."

"Do you mean to say," said Lord Guy wrathfully, "that you wormed your way into my household to *spy* on me?"

"No, no, no!" wailed Manuel. "I wish to write like Monsieur Cavet. Please look at his articles. . . ."

"My stupid fellow, I have no time to look into your journalistic ambitions at the moment. Now, what did you say to Miss Jones?"

Manuel hung his head. "I think if you marry her, you no go back to Portugal. I must go to Portugal to continue my writings. So I tell her you laugh about her and say you trick her."

Lord Guy signalled to Rainbird to step forward. "What do you do with me?" cried Manuel.

"I do nothing with you until I find Miss Jones and get her to marry me."

Lord Guy turned to Rainbird. "This man is to be locked in the cellar," he said. "I will decide what to do with him when I return. In the meanwhile, Manuel, I will keep your notebook and these newspapers. Tommy, go with Rainbird and keep Manuel covered with your gun. When he is locked up, prepare to come with me to Brighton. We'll take the vicar with us!"

Miss Fipps tried several times on the road to Brighton to get Esther to explain why she had rushed off from London. Esther stubbornly said over and over again that the children would be better removed from the danger of the mob, and although that seemed very sensible, she looked so miserable and white as she said it that Miss Fipps came gloomily to the conclusion that Something Terrible had happened between Miss Jones and Carlton during the night.

Amy and Peter were fortunately still at the age when they considered all adult behaviour incalculable and as little subject to reason as that of the ancient Greek gods. Foremost in their minds was the thought they were going to see the sea for the first time in their lives.

As they neared Brighton and the children were screaming with delight at the sight of the grey sea lying below them, Miss Fipps asked timidly, "Where do you intend to stay, Miss Jones? At an hotel?"

"No," said Esther. "I shall find a house."

"Perhaps there will not be one to rent," ventured Miss Fipps timidly.

"Then I shall buy one," said Esther.

Miss Fipps sighed. How wonderful to have so much money that it was a matter of indifference whether one rented a house or bought it.

She did not know that Esther, normally thrifty, cared for her wealth only in that it might supply some means of material comfort to ease the bruising her soul had received at Lord Guy's hands.

Miss Fipps was feeling tired and slightly sick from the swaying of the carriage. She was sure they would search until nightfall for a house and finally end up at an hotel.

But no sooner had they arrived in Brighton than Esther sent her footmen off to find out agents with houses for sale or rent. By an hour's time, she had taken possession of an elegant house on the Steyne, renting it and its servants for a month—the owners, who had not expected to find a tenant until the summer, being so overwhelmed with a generous offer of hard cash that they had promptly moved out and inflicted themselves on their relations for the month.

Standing in the middle of a pretty drawing-room, Esther rapped out orders like a general. The carriage was to return to London and bring the rest of the luggage from Berkeley Square. The new maid, Charlotte, was to accompany the baggage so that she might begin her training under Esther's eye. Fires were to be lit in all the rooms. Accompanied by the housekeeper, Esther walked through the bedrooms examining the linen to make sure it was dry and aired, the cellars to see they were properly stocked, and the kitchens to make sure there was a sufficient quantity of food.

It was getting on for six in the evening. The children were clamouring for a walk by the sea, and Esther, frightened to let herself sit down and think, said she would take them.

It was a chilly spring evening as she walked on the pebbly beach with the children running before her. The waves advanced and retreated, moving the shingle back and forward with a sad, sighing sound. The sun was setting, laying out a long golden path across the sea from shore to horizon.

How wonderful it would be, thought Esther wretchedly, to walk into that golden path and keep on walking until the sea covered her head, that cropped head which the fickle and philandering Lord Guy had not liked.

When she saw the figures of two men approaching from the distance, along the beach, she called sharply to the children. She was not accompanied by a maid or footman and did not want two bucks to take her for a governess or nursery maid, not knowing that the richness of her new wardrobe and the stern haughty look on her face made such a mistake nigh impossible.

But Peter and Amy appeared deaf to her calls as they ran and played and shouted to each other.

She called again, more sharply. But to her horror, the children were now running towards the two approaching figures. One was tall and slim and elegant, and the other, short and swarthy.

With a fast-beating heart, Esther recognised Lord Guy and Mr. Roger.

The sudden hope in her heart made her feel sick.

Amy and Peter had reached Lord Guy. He was laughing down at them. He ruffled Peter's red curls, and then, holding each child by the hand, he continued to walk towards Esther.

When he came up to her, he was laughing at something Peter had said, but the gaze he turned on Esther was stern and cold.

He held up his hand as she began to speak, and said, "Tommy, take the children back to the house and tell them what is to happen this evening. Children, we are to have something of a party, and you must wear your best clothes and be on your best behaviour."

"A party!" screamed Amy in delight. "What is it for?"

"That is a secret," he said. "If you go now and if you are very good, perhaps Mr. Roger will tell you."

"You cannot come down here and start ordering my brother and sister about," cried Esther.

But Amy and Peter were already dancing off beside Mr. Roger, plying him with excited questions.

He waited until they were out of earshot and then turned to Esther.

"You owe me an explanation, madam," he said.

"I owe *you* an explanation!" said Esther.

"Why did you run away? I had a time of it finding you. I tried all the hotels and inns and finally roused the agents. I discovered your house just when I had nigh become sick and tired of looking for it."

"You came to look for me," said Esther in wonder.

"Madam, I am not in the habit of visiting Brighton out of season for any normal reason. Why did you leave? What did Manuel say?"

"Your servant? He told me you had been . . . laughing . . . about how you had tricked me."

"Manuel, it appears, is a budding journalist, a fool and probably quite mad."

"A journalist!"

"The silly idiot thought to make a name for himself in an American newspaper, like some French journalist called Cavet. Alas, for poor Manuel! This Cavet writes as if he had obtained a post in a noble household and goes on to describe scandalous happenings in the household. But it is all fiction. Only Manuel could believe that someone called Lord Pink really existed. The articles were translated into French and published in the French papers, which is where Manuel first read them. This journal, the *Sun*, went so far as to encourage him in his folly by suggesting in a letter written to Manuel a year ago that he confine his reports to that of a servant at war. He evidently tried to pass his time in London by taking notes of troop movements."

"He is despicable!" said Esther.

"I do not know what to do with him now. I studied the drafts of some of his articles on the journey here. Amazingly enough, apart from occasional lapses into bad English, he writes extremely well. The descriptions of Portugal were so vivid I could almost fancy myself back there. I have him locked in the cellar in Clarges Street. But now we have disposed of Manuel, the question remains why you believed such a farrago of nonsense."

"Your reputation," said Esther, hanging her head. "My father played such a trick once on a girl, made love to her and ruined her. She did not know he was married."

" 'Fore God, Esther, I am unwed, and I am not your father, and your own reputation is now somewhat soiled."

"I do not have your experience of love affairs," said Esther, blinking tears from her eyes.

He sighed wearily and turned away from her and looked out to sea.

"I should not have distrusted you," said Esther shakily. "I had always thought myself intelligent and sensible. But I am so confused. The world of the ton has different moral laws from my own private world."

He turned back to her. "We are wasting time. Come. I have brought the vicar with me. We must be married while he is still sober."

"Married? Do you feel you *have* to marry me?"

"Yes," he said baldly. He made no move to take her in his arms and his eyes were as cold as the darkening sea.

"Then I will not marry you," said Esther. "Consider yourself free."

He drew a pistol from his pocket and levelled it at her.

"You are going to marry me and no one else, Esther, so start walking back to that house you have rented as quickly as possible."

Esther gave a nervous laugh. "May I point out that it is the man who is usually forced to marry at gunpoint?"

"I am in no mood for jesting," he said coldly. "March."

So Esther marched, her thoughts in a miserable turmoil. All her initial hope and elation at seeing him was dying away. Although he might have led a scandalous life,

Lord Guy was as much a member of the ton as Mr. Brummell. Where she stumbled, he moved with easy grace through the peculiar ways of society. He had stayed alone with her, he had kissed her in public. He felt he had to marry her.

He had moved next to her and taken her arm in a strong grip, speaking only once to remind her he had the gun in his pocket.

"Why is Esther looking so white and miserable?" whispered Amy to Miss Fipps.

"Bride nerves," said Miss Fipps. "All ladies look thus at their wedding."

Reassured, Amy clutched her little nosegay of flowers and prepared to take her place behind Esther at the "altar" —an escritoire draped in red velvet that had been set up at the end of the drawing-room. The vicar, the Reverend Abraham Pascombe, seemed to be in a state of suppressed fury, which indeed he was. He had never felt so sober in his life. Neither Mr. Roger nor Lord Guy had allowed him anything stronger than coffee, saying he could drink as much as he liked after the ceremony was over. He drawled and droned his way through the wedding service until he heard the jolly sound of a cork being pulled coming from the dining room across the hall, where the servants were preparing the wedding supper. He brightened perceptibly and rattled through the rest of the proceedings with an almost indecent haste.

In all her misery and bewilderment, Esther could reflect only that there was a lot to be said for the efficiency of an army man combined with the talents of Miss Fipps. How had they managed to find, not only a bouquet for herself, but a nosegay for Amy, and huge vases of flowers for the room at such short notice? She stumbled her way through the responses, pausing only to raise her eyebrows when she thought she heard the vicar mumble, "Oh, get on with it, do!"

No sooner were she and Lord Guy pronounced man and wife than the double doors leading to the hall were thrown open and a small orchestra, magically found by Mr. Roger and dragged from a nearby hotel, began to play the wedding march.

At the supper, Mr. Roger toasted the health of the bride and bridegroom. Mellowed with wine, the vicar got to his feet and made his speech, which was surprisingly urbane and witty. He was at that stage where he had drunk enough to be clever and not yet enough to become maudlin. Lord Guy made a graceful speech. He considered himself the happiest of men, he said, looking down at his bride thoughtfully, as if measuring her for her coffin.

Esther, unused to much wine, drank a great deal. At first it worked, giving her a feeling of elation, making her feel sure he really loved her and was not just doing what he considered to be his duty.

But as the supper drew to its close and the tired children were taken upstairs to the nursery, she found she was becoming sober again. And very frightened.

At last, it was time to go upstairs to bed with her lord. Miss Fipps cried a little and kissed Esther warmly. Mr. Roger kissed her as well and then held back the vicar, who was advancing on Esther with a lustful gleam in his eye.

Lord Guy held out his arm and escorted Esther from the room.

They stood and faced each other in the hall. Esther was wearing a white silk slip with an overdress of silver net held with silver clasps. On her red curls gleamed a diamond tiara, Miss Fipps having pointed out that when it came to weddings, diamonds were not "exploded." It was a gown she had chosen to wear for her début at Almack's. She would never see the inside of Almack's now, she reflected inconsequentially.

She looked up at him bravely. "Now you have done your duty, my lord," she said, "I bid you good night."

A wicked smile curled his lips. "My love and my life," he mocked, "I have not even begun to do my duty."

He swept her up in his arms, carrying her as easily as if she had been Amy and not a strapping woman of nearly six feet.

"Don't struggle," he said, as he carried her up the stairs. "I am still quite prepared to shoot you."

"I don't know where my bedroom is," pleaded Esther. "I have forgotten."

"You will sleep in mine." He kicked open a door and carried her into a spacious bedroom and tossed her on the bed. Her sparkling tiara rolled off her head and clattered onto the floor.

"Guy . . . please," she begged as he began to rip off his clothes.

"Esther, I am still very angry with you. Do not make me more angry, I beg."

As his small-clothes followed the rest of his clothes, Esther put her hands over her eyes. There was a creak as he climbed on the bed. He jerked down her hands and crouched over her. The room was in darkness, lit only by the flames of the fire, which sent a red glow over his lean, muscled, naked body.

"Now you," he said, reaching for the clasps of her dress.

"Not like this," said Esther miserably. "Not like this, my lord. You go on as if you were about to punish me."

He gave a soft laugh. "Oh, my love, do you not realise how angry you make me? I hate it when you look at me with

161

those large, terrified eyes. Here, let me hold you. It will be all right. Everything will be all right."

He began to kiss her slowly and caressingly, the inexperienced Esther not knowing what great a rein he was keeping on his emotions. He kissed her until he felt her begin to respond. He held her tightly against the length of his naked body, enduring the discomfort of silver clasps digging into his skin until he felt her body turn pliant and eager under his touch. Esther never could understand afterwards how he managed to remove all her clothes without her being aware of it. Then his voice in her ear said, "This is going to hurt a little. Hold me tightly and remember I love you more than life itself."

That wonderful statement of love carried Esther over the pain and bewilderment of losing her virginity. When he was ready to take her again, she melted into his arms, burning with passion, knowing at last what he meant about there being another kind of burning. The third time he had her, she did not know where he began or she ended, either physically or mentally.

At last, during the long length of a lazy morning punctuated with languid kisses and uninhibited caresses, Esther said softly, "What happens now? Do we stay in Brighton?"

"For a few days," he said. "We will travel to Yorkshire to stay with my parents and make arrangements for Peter and Amy. We will be married again in my family chapel."

"But what of the house in Clarges Street? What will you do with that?"

"Forget it," he said. "I paid for the whole Season in advance. The servants there are so self-sufficient, they will do very well without me."

"And Manuel?"

Lord Guy began to laugh. "Do you know what I am going to do with Manuel? I am going to send that ambitious little writer enough money to take himself back to Portugal. He deserves to be punished for his folly, but I no longer have the heart to do so."

"Rainbird. He never replied to my offer."

"He won't leave the others. Do you know, I was getting jealous of that fellow. It always seemed to be Rainbird says this, and Rainbird says that. But I am indebted to him for his masterly idea of a children's party. Had he not hit on the idea of me rescuing you, I perhaps would never have been able to hold you in my arms and kiss you like this . . . and this . . ."

"You mean," said Esther when she could, "that the whole party was a plot?"

But he did not reply. Instead his lips moved to her breast. Clarges Street, Rainbird, Lizzie, and all the rest whirled away in a delicious warm blackness as rake and reformer set out once more to explore each other.

Chapter
Eleven

The insatiate itch of scribbling.

—WILLIAM GIFFORD

Rainbird walked back to Clarges Street after another futile visit to Berkeley Square. Graves, the butler, jealous and suspicious of Rainbird, refused to give him any news of his mistress, and this last visit had slammed the door in his face.

Where were all the lucrative ton parties they had expected Lord Guy to give? thought Rainbird. One Cyprian debauch could hardly be said to qualify as a London society event.

He had been sorely tempted to accept Esther's offer, if only to put Graves in his place. And yet, thought Rainbird, determined to be fair, he himself would take it badly were some other butler to usurp his position in Clarges Street.

Joseph greeted him when he arrived in the servants' hall.

"Looks like a packet from my lord," said Joseph. "Come by the morning post, it did."

"Remarkably quiet down there," said Rainbird, glancing down at the floor. Manuel had been shouting and screaming for the whole week of his incarceration. He broke open the seal.

His face fell as he read the contents. The others clustered around. "My lord," said Rainbird heavily, "married Miss Jones in Brighton. But," he went on, "he is not returning to London. He has given me a draft to his bank for our wages until the end of the Season and also enough to enable two of us to take Manuel to the coast and put him on a ship. It seems that wretched man is to be rewarded by being sent back to Portugal to continue his writing. Let's hope he turns out to be a good writer, for he has proved to be a bad servant."

"That's very good news, Mr. Rainbird," said Lizzie, who was secretly sorry for Manuel. "And to pay our wages is very handsome. And perhaps Mr. Palmer will find us another tenant. The Season has only just begun."

"I had hoped for parties," said Rainbird. "Good pickings to be had during the Season. Oh, well, surely the bad luck of this house is at an end. No one's been killed or ruined lately. There is also a letter from Lady Guy. She says . . . let me see . . . if I still wish a post in her employ, to write to her . . . she gives the Earl of Cramworth's direction in Yorkshire."

"You weren't thinking of leaving us!" cried Lizzie in distress.

"No," said Rainbird crossly, "but you were."

"That was different," said Lizzie, hanging her head. "I didn't rightly know what I was doing then."

"What else does she say?" asked Dave.

"She says she is grateful to me for everything and her only regret is that she ruined her reputation. Well, that's saved, thanks to my lord."

Before he had left London for Brighton, Lord Guy had given Rainbird a short letter to copy and deliver to all the

165

newspapers. It carried a spirited account of Esther's rescue of Charlotte. The newspapers, glad to have something cheerful to report now that the mob had been brought to heel, had published it. Prints had subsequently appeared in booksellers' windows showing Esther as a stern figure of Britannia, clutching Charlotte to her side, and lecturing decadent society on its evil ways.

"I'd better take the cratur doon some food," said Angus. "Shall I tell him the good news—that he's to go to Portugal?"

"I'll come with you," said Rainbird. "Manuel is unnaturally quiet. He may be waiting behind the cellar door to attack us. I still think you ought to have bound him, Angus."

"He's nae match for the likes o' me," said the cook.

Angus put a plate of sliced beef, some bread and pickle, and a small tankard of beer on a tray. Rainbird put down the letters and lit a candle and followed the cook to the head of the cellar steps.

"It *is* very quiet down there," said Rainbird uneasily. "Let me go in first, Angus."

He walked down the cellar steps and stood listening for a moment. Then he put the candle on the floor by the door, unlocked it, and let it swing open.

Silence.

"Manuel," called Rainbird.

"Shine the light," said Angus.

Rainbird raised the candle and shone it into the cellar.

Manuel was sitting at a table, his head lolling back and his eyes closed.

"Saints preserve us," whispered Angus behind him. "The man's dead."

Rainbird's hand holding the candle began to shake.

"It's this damned house!" he cried. "It's haunted.

Death, nothing but death and violence! It means to keep us here, Angus. It'll keep us here until we rot."

A plaintive little voice said, "I am not dead. I wish I were."

"Manuel!" cried Rainbird, nearly crying with relief. "You are free and we have good news for you. Come upstairs."

He and Angus MacGregor led Manuel out of his cellar-prison and up to the servants' hall, where the others were all gathered.

Rainbird found Manuel a seat at the table and gave him back his notebook, cuttings, and letters, which Lord Guy had included with his letter.

Then he told him slowly and carefully that my lord had sent money so that Manuel might be able to return to Portugal to continue his writing.

Manuel looked around in a dazed way. "Me, I am to be set free?" he asked.

"Yes," said Angus curtly. He was rapidly getting over his relief at finding Manuel alive.

Manuel's black eyes began to shine. "It must be because milord thinks I am the good writer. Here! I shall read to you."

He began to read out a report of life in Portugal. Angus started caustically to correct Manuel's English, but when the servant did not take offence but only listened intently and marked down the corrections, the cook became enthusiastic. He drew up a chair beside Manuel and listened with growing interest.

"I must say," said the cook, scratching his red head when Manuel had finished, "that you have a fine turn o' phrase. But that doesn't change ma mind about ye. I still think you are not a very pleasant character, you with your knives and all those nasty things you wrote about us in that book o' yours."

Manuel spread his hands. "I only wrote those things because I knew you were suspicious and might search my room. Life has not been easy. The other English servants in the barracks, they were cruel to me. I decide I despise English servants. But not now. You forgive me?"

The others looked at each other doubtfully, but Lizzie had enjoyed Manuel's writing and was relieved he was free. "Yes, we do," she said. "Fancy you being a Frenchman. If you wasn't French, we'd get you to show us some of them Spanish dances we heard of."

"I know them," cried Manuel, leaping up. "See, I show you. I have not the castanets, but perhaps two spoons . . . ?"

Joseph fetched his mandolin and Angus produced two spoons. "I don't know if I've got this right," said Joseph cautiously, strumming some opening chords.

Soon Manuel was nimbly leaping about, clacking the spoons like castanets.

"Now the lady's part," he said, seizing Alice by the hand. "And she must have a lace mantilla."

Laughing, Jenny produced a lace curtain from her workbasket and they pinned it on Alice's golden hair.

The others laughed and applauded as Alice moved through the steps of the dance at her usual slow pace, amiably submitting to Manuel's teaching.

Rainbird, feeling suddenly depressed, slipped out of the room and went upstairs to be by himself.

Was the house really unlucky? Here they were at the beginning of the Season without a tenant. But their wages were to be paid and that was something to be thankful for. . . . From downstairs came a high cackle of laughter. Manuel. Well, hearing Manuel laugh at last was surely a miracle.

Miracles did happen. They had had a great deal of unexpected good fortune during the past few years. Soon they would have their freedom, soon they would be the masters and not the servants. All it would take was a little more time, and a little more luck.

Feeling cheerful again, Rainbird went back downstairs to join the party.

Enchanting Regency Romances

A LONDON SEASON by Anthea Bell
There's malice, mystery and merriment as two lively ladies set Regency society astir!

_____ 90234-4 $3.95 U.S.

RAMILLIES by Barbara Whitehead
A shy young earl must choose a bride, but his heart is given to two beauties.

_____ 90512-2 $2.95 U.S.

LADYSMEAD by Jane Gillespie
Sophia was almost resigned to a quiet life in the country when love surprised her.

_____ 90490-8 $2.95 U.S.

TEVERTON HALL by Jane Gillespie
She was only the daughter of the rector, yet she'd lost her heart to the heir to Teverton Hall.

_____ 90674-9 $2.95 U.S.

THE MISER OF MAYFAIR by Marion Chesney
The delightful first volume of the new series, A House for the Season, by one of the superstars of the Regency Romance.

_____ 90689-7 $2.95 U.S.

PUBLISHERS BOOK AND AUDIO MAILING SERVICE
594 Foster Road
Staten Island, NY 10309

Please send me the book(s) I have checked above. I am enclosing a check or money order (not cash) for $_____ plus $1.00 for the first book plus $.25 for each additional book to cover postage and handling (New York residents add applicable sales tax).

Name _____

Address _____

City _____ State _____ Zip Code _____

Allow at least 4 to 6 weeks for delivery